MW00457061

Memoirs of an Unproud Man

Victor Norber

DEDICATION

To my late wife, Jo and my children, Elaine, Sue
and Steven

CONTENTS

ACKNOWLEDGMENTS

In 1974, I decided to write my memoirs as a legacy to my children. In 2000, I finished my story. It was not a struggle writing it; I was busy doing other things.

Seven years later, my beloved wife and soul mate for 51 years passed away. Shortly before she died she asked to get back to my book, add a couple of chapters, a new ending and send it to a publisher. I promised I would.

My daughter, Elaine Boyd, in 2008 typed my entire 65,000 word story. Considering she was working eight hours a day, actively engaged in church and social functions with her husband, she found time to produce this prodigious work of mine meant only one thing to me. She loved her aging father very much. I will always be grateful to Elaine for this marvelous accomplishment. She was my typist extraordinaire.

In 2010, Bill Fleischman became my editor. He rearranged several chapters, putting them in chronological order. Were it not for Elaine and Bill, there would be no book legacy. His was work invaluable in preparing my text.

Also invaluable in the preparation of my text were two highly skilled , eagle-eyed proofreaders, Mary Gasich and Rachel Wease, who corrected many of my punctuation errors.

I would also thank my other expert typists, Jeanne Schott and Katherine Strawhun, who took over for me when my own typing ability failed me at age 90.

PREFACE

Twenty-two months after the close of World War II in Europe, an entire combat command, including attached units, was awarded the Presidential Unit Citation for action that occurred in the Hurtgen Forest of Germany in late November and early December 1944.

The citation dated 18 March 1947 was long overdue in coming. Most unit citations were awarded as soon as possible following the commendable action – usually within six months to a year.

The fierce battle of the Hurtgen Forest, which cost this command 50 of its 58 tanks and 680 of its 750 infantrymen, is, conservatively put, relatively unknown.

DISTINGUISHED UNIT CITATIONS
COMBAT COMMAND R
TROOP A, 85th CAVALRY RECONNAISSANCE SQUADRON (MECZ)
COMPANY B, 47th ARMORED INFANTRY BATTALION
COMPANY C, 47th ARMORED INFANTRY BATTALION

COMBAT COMMAND R AT KLEINHAU, BRANDENBURG, AND BERGSTEIN

GENERAL ORDERS }   WAR DEPARTMENT
No. 31   }   WASHINGTON 25, D. C., 18 March 1947

*   *   *   *   *

I. — *BATTLE HONORS.* — As authorized by Executive Order 9396 (sec. I, WD Bul. 22, 1943), superseding Executive Order 9075 (sec. III, WD Bul. II, 1942), the following units are cited by the War Department under the provisions of section IV, WD Circular 333, 1943, in the name of the President of the United States as public evidence of deserved honor and distinction. The citation reads as follows:

Combat Command R, 5th Armored Division, composed of the following units:
  Headquarters Reserve Command, 5th Armored Division;
  Detachment A, Headquarters and Headquarters Company, 3d Armored Group;
  10th Tank Battalion;
  47th Armored Infantry Battalion;
  95th Armored Field Artillery Battalion;
  Company C, 85th Cavalry Reconnaissance Squadron (Mecz);
  Company C, 22d Armored Engineer Battalion;
  Company C, 628th Tank Destroyer Battalion (SP);
  Company C, 387th Antiaircraft (AW) Battalion (SP);
  Company C, 75th Medical Battalion (Armored);
  Detachment, Company C, 127th Ordnance Maintenance Battalion,

is cited for outstanding performance of duty in action from 29 November to 8 December 1944 in Germany. During the severe battle of the Hurtgen Forest, this combat command played a heroic and highly essential part in the operation aimed at capturing the vital Roer River dams. *Combat Command R, 5th Armored Division*, spearheaded three important advances during the period, capturing Kleinhau on 29 November, Brandenberg on 3 December, and Bergstein on 5 December. In each instance, the men of *Combat Command R, 5th Armored Division*, were sent out front to capture the fortified town and hold it until friendly infantry could clear the adjacent woods. Under extremely unfavorable weather conditions and over terrain emphatically not suited to armored action, this command gallantly attacked through deadly mine fields against a determined enemy, well-entrenched, fortified, and supported by intense artillery and mortar fire. In conjunction with friendly infantry on the flanks, *Combat Command R, 5th Armored Division*, successfully captured the three important towns and cleared a fortified zone of enemy resistance on the Vossenach Ridge. Since Bergstein was most important to the Germans in connection with the defense of the Roer River dams, they defended it bitterly and made fanatic efforts to recapture it, once it had fallen. However, *Combat Command R, 5th Armored Division*, although reduced to 8 effective tanks and some 20 effective riflemen per company, employed the last available man, and heroically repelled almost continuous combined armored and infantry counterattacks against the heights of Bergstein for a period of 56 hours. In keeping with the highest traditions of the military service, the entire *Combat Command R, 5th Armored Division*, and attached units, by its undaunted determination, outstanding courage, and grim tenacity, captured and held, against the strongest German resistance, the important heights which dominated the Roer River dams.

2

THE GENERAL, THE CAPTAIN AND JOE

Having assisted in the planning of the North African Invasion and having successfully led a combat command of the United States 1st Armored Division in the early fighting of the North African Campaign, Major General Lunsford E. Oliver had been ordered to return to the States, where he would be rewarded with the command of an entire armored division: the United States 5th Armored Division.

Before leaving Africa, General Oliver picked two battle-wise officers from the battlefields of North Africa to accompany him to his new assignment. The officers were a Captain Cannon and a Lieutenant Pool.

In early March 1943, on a reviewing platform that stood on the parade grounds of Camp Cooke, California, General Oliver officially took command of the United States 5th Armored Division. After being introduced to his new troops that were assembled before him on the parade grounds, the general turned to his aides, Captain Cannon and Lieutenant Pool, and introduced them to the division.

From my view in formation, some thirty feet from the platform, I could see the features of all three men on the stand quite clearly. And my heart swelled with pride as I stared at them, for I knew these were battle-hardened officers, leaders fresh from the battlefields of North Africa, men

3

of courage and honor; brilliant men destined to lead us to victory when it was our turn to go to battle.

A few days after this inaugural ceremony took place in California, our division moved to Tennessee, where it was to participate in Tennessee maneuvers.

On a muddy spring day, shortly after we had set up camp in Tennessee, I walked into the Company Orderly Room expecting to talk to the first sergeant about some minor detail he wanted to discuss with me. On entering, I was surprised and pleased to find Captain Frank Pool, formerly Lieutenant Pool, aide to General Oliver, standing in the center of the orderly room talking with our first sergeant. On being introduced to the captain, I learned that he was now our new company commander.

With our new commander, came the rumor that the general was keeping his eye on this battle-proven officer and though the general had arranged for his promotion and assignment to our company, he thought as highly of his former aide as he did of anyone on his personal staff. "Don't think the colonels on the general's staff outrank this captain," we heard, "he got the general's attention in Africa and he's still got it." So went the rumor. A rumor I soon believed.

That the story was substantially true would become crystal clear to me some seventeen months later. For it was on a day in mid-September of 1944 that I would observe a small reconnaissance patrol, consisting of three tanks and an open-air peep making its way through a series of concrete pillboxes that were strung out along the German frontier. *(In the armored forces, jeeps were known as peeps).* Sitting in the peep was General Oliver, and on his left, just a few feet away, was Captain Pool, standing tall in the turret of his tank. On the other side of the general, and standing tall in the turret of his own tank, was Staff Sergeant Joe Verhagen, new leader of the captain's third platoon. Slightly to the rear of these three vehicles, which appeared to be on line, there could be seen a trailing vehicle; an insurance tank that had gone along for extra lookout and increased firepower.

Because Intelligence had been sketchy regarding German strength in this area of the West Wall (The Siegfried Line) and uncertainty existed as to whether or not the concrete pillboxes were manned. They were not. The general decided that he himself should personally investigate the area. To accompany him on this highly important and perhaps dangerous mission, the general had chosen Captain Pool. In turn, Captain Pool had chosen Staff Sergeant Joe Verhagen, his battle-proven leader of the third platoon, to accompany them. (In organizing the patrol, the captain had Joe pick the insurance tank from the third platoon.)

Shortly after the information gathered on this reconnaissance mission was evaluated, the 5th Armored Division invaded Germany at Wallendorf, and it was there that our first clash with German forces on their own soil would take place.

Seeing firsthand the general's trust in the captain on the reconnaissance mission, convinced me that I had been right in believing the rumor about the captain when he first came to our company. Knowing Captain Pool had chosen Joe to accompany them on this vital mission, I believed that perhaps the captain saw in Joe what the general saw in the captain.

How did I see and know so much about the Wallendorf recon? I was there. I was Joe's gunner.

In retrospect, however, I need to return to when Captain Pool first arrived.

LIEUTENANT P.B.Y.

Captain Frank Pool came to us in the early Spring 1943. In taking over our company, the captain was not inheriting a bunch of raw recruits or ill-trained men, but rather he was getting men who had gone through eight months of intensive Army training at Camp Cooke, California, as well as having gone through four months of mock battles in the Mojave Desert. (Indeed, while on desert maneuvers, two artillery units were withdrawn from our division and sent to North Africa, where they fought in that campaign.)

In my fourteenth month of unspectacular military service, I was a Technician Fifth Grade (T/5) radio-tender medium tank crewman. Though all I did with the radio was turn the transmitter and receiver on and off, I was rated as a "technician" because I performed my work in a platoon leader's tank. In addition to my radio duties, I also loaded the 75mm and 30 caliber co-axially mounted machine gun when out on the firing range; and since this was to be my main job in combat, I was also referred to as a "loader".

Having flawlessly flipped the "on-off" toggle switches on the transmitter and receiver in a Platoon Leader tank for the past seven or eight months, my record as a radio-tender in a lead tank was undoubtedly spotless, and for that reason, I supposed, Captain Pool, who as yet knew none of us personally, assigned me to be part of a newly put together crew that was to man the lead tank of the second platoon.

The enlisted men in the crew of Two-One (second platoon, first tank) had pretty much the same military background. We had come into the Army a little over a year ago and all of us had received our basic training and follow-up tank training in the same company. The lieutenant who was assigned to command our tank was another story. Fresh out of Officer Candidate School, his experiences in the Armored Force were limited to what he had learned in ninety days of schooling. After telling us he'd come directly from school to us, our new commander went on to say that previous to his schooling, he had served in the Navy. It seems he had been a Naval Air Corps pilot and had been stationed on an aircraft carrier when he suddenly developed landing problems that led to a shortening of his career as a pilot. More specifically, on two occasions when attempting to land his plane on the flight deck of the carrier, he inadvertently slammed into the side of the carrier. The Navy, after plucking him from the pond the second time, washed him out. An Ex-pilot, he now decided he'd like to try tanks. So he joined the Army, went to Officer Candidate School, got his commission, and was promptly assigned to our outfit so he could get some much needed field experience.

After hearing his troubles in the Navy, our new tank crew hoped and believed he would find his experiences with tanks far more rewarding than his experiences with planes had been.

Interestingly enough, even after he'd been with us for a week or two and could see that we all liked and respected him as our commander and a tanker, he still maintained a strong spiritual attachment to planes. There were times when the lieutenant would be talking with us when the sound of an airplane could be heard overhead, and the lieutenant, casting his eyes skyward, would most reverently say, "Did you know that Alexander P.D. Seversky says in his book, Victory Through Air Power, that the war could be won through the use of air power alone?"

As a result of his attachment to planes, the new tank leader of the second platoon quickly became known as Lieutenant P.B.Y., which initials were the designation of a Naval reconnaissance seaplane. Of course, no one ever addressed him as Lieutenant P.B.Y., for doing so would have been as rewarding as addressing General Patton as General "Blood and Guts."

On an evening in late April, two weeks after Lieutenant P.B.Y. joined us, Tennessee Maneuvers got underway. Problem One was a scheduled dusk to dawn operation, which meant that most of the movement of tanks and infantry would be carried out under cover of darkness. Our company's mission in Problem One was to destroy "enemy forces" which were situated beyond a very wide and deep forest that stood facing us. In our briefing, we were told the manner in which we were to negotiate this forest. At dusk, our second platoon would make the initial jump, moving into the forest and swinging left. Immediately afterwards the first platoon would enter the forest swinging right, and at the same time the third platoon would head straight into the forest. These movements were to be carried out in the fading daylight hours, when "enemy" observers could spot us. (Obviously these tactics were made to confuse them.) Much later, after night had fallen and our platoons had gone their separate ways into the darkened forest, instructions would be radioed to the platoons telling them to meet at a designated area (rendezvous point) in the forest. After rendezvousing with our company and other elements in our regiment, our now unified force would proceed the rest of the way through the forest, and on emerging from the trees we would assault and overcome the "enemy" who would no doubt be caught napping.

It sounded like a simple and clever plan, which included the wonderful elements of surprise and enemy confusion. Keenly aware that much of the execution depended on good radio communication, I thoroughly checked my radio and equipment several hours prior to jumping-off time.

In the lengthening evening shadows of that April "D-Day" evening, as Lieutenant P.B.Y. was leading our second platoon through the forest, I was sitting by the radio hearing the voice of the lieutenant coming clearly over the intercom, giving instructions to our driver, Bill Aldy. No outside communication could be heard because at this state of the operation we were traveling in radio silence.

As night fell, darkness covered the forest, and our tanks moved stealthily through the trees; the sounds of tree branches scraping against the outside armor of our tank could be heard clearly and distinctly inside our turret. Except for an occasional interruption by the lieutenant in issuing a terse order to our driver, we traveled silently.

Presently the captain's voice came in, "Black One (command tank) to Two One, your location. Over."

Responding to the Two One call, Lieutenant P.B.Y. pressed down on his mike button and gave the captain our coordinates.

A few seconds passed and the captain called again, repeating his request.

Realizing the lieutenant might not have gotten out, I signaled the gunner across from me to look at the lieutenant's control box to make sure he had switched his toggle switch to "out." On "out" the gunner signaled. Turning my attention to the transmitter dial, I saw that the needle failed to rise when he pressed his mike button.

"Blew a fuse!" I yelled to the lieutenant, and after quickly inserting a spare fuse, I signaled him to press down on his mike button again. He pressed down his mike button and as he did, I saw the needle on the dial flip up momentarily only to fall back to zero in a split second.

"Damn fuse blew again!" I yelled to the lieutenant, and after quickly inserting another spare fuse, I signaled him to transmit. He pressed down on his mike button, and the fuse blew again.

And so it went; and while we were blowing fuses, the captain's voice was becoming more and more faint. Finally, it was heard no more. We had gone out of his radio range.

After traveling among the trees for what seemed an eternity, we finally came back to a clearing of some sort. The sound of the tree branches scraping against the tank had ceased and light from overhead, not moonlight, came pouring in through the turret opening. Very cautiously, I moved over to the gunner's side of the turret and poked my head up through the turret opening. A strange sight greeted me. We were rumbling down the main drag of a little town and the light that was coming into our turret came from the street lights that lined the main street in downtown Manchester, Tennessee.

Looking behind, I saw the remaining four tanks of our platoon following closely in single file. As we paraded down the well-lit thoroughfare, crowds of townspeople began gathering at the curbs pointing at us and staring, and some, it seemed to me, were laughing, wondering where we had come from. And the thought occurred to me that we had assaulted and successfully invaded a peaceful community that lay several miles outside the maneuver perimeter.

For all of us in the second platoon, Problem One was over.

On the following day, Problem One ended for the rest of our regiment and our platoon was ordered to proceed to the regroup area where we would rejoin the other tanks in our company. Waiting there to talk with me were two communications sergeants from regimental headquarters. This duo, known as "General Do-Little" and "Major Does-Less", because they had so little to do in performing their daily jobs, had serviced the radio in my tank shortly after I had checked it and shortly before we jumped off on Problem One. I remembered well the last time I saw them.

13

I had been standing by my tank when these two sergeants had approached me. "Regimental headquarters sent us to do a last minute check on your radio because you guys are gonna lead off at kickoff," the Tech Staff Sergeant, General Do-Little, said, The buck Sergeant, General Does-Less, nodded yes, confirming it was an official visit.

I saw no reason for the check-up. I'd never once had a problem with the radio, so as I watched them scramble up the side of the tank and disappear into the turret, I figured the officers back at headquarters just wanted to give these guys some work practice so their talents wouldn't rust out.

After spending two or three minutes in the turret puttering around with the radio, the sergeants emerged and informed me that they found everything working perfectly. They indicated particular care was taken to see that my fuses were good. "Never have any trouble with these sets outside a blown fuse, so we took your old set of spares and replaced them with a new set. And we also put a new fuse in your transmitter."

I thanked them for being so conscientious in servicing the radio, and they went on their way.

What they neglected to tell me was that they had replaced ½ amp fuses with ¼ amp fuses.

Now, as they were standing with me in the regroup area explaining how they had happened to erroneously grab the wrong fuses, the Staff Sergeant was taking the full blame saying, "Never made a mistake like this before in my entire life. I feel awful about this."

In accepting his apology, I pointed out that the blame for the foul-up was all mine, because it was my responsibility to check my equipment after any servicing and this I had failed to do.

In looking back on everything that had occurred on that fouled-up mission, I realized that I wasn't the only one who had screwed up. At the first sign of trouble with our transmitter, the lieutenant could have switched tanks and gone to the Platoon Sergeant's tank which is also equipped with a transmitter and maintained communication and assumed command from that tank. Unfortunately, at the time of the breakdown, the idea of switching tanks never occurred to either of us.

Although the incident was considered closed by our crew, who felt the less said about it the better, there were others in our company who, seeing the humorous side of the "Tennessee Invasion," refused to let the incident die. One tanker from another platoon came up with, "Is it true when you guys were parading in Manchester the other night, just as you were passing a picture show you stuck your head through the turret and said to the lieutenant, "Hmmm, I wonder what's on the show tonight?" (This particular joke actually took on a rumor aspect and weeks later some tankers outside our own company asked me if I'd really said that.) One clever tanker came up with, "I hear Lieutenant P.B.Y. has a new name, now he's Lieutenant Manchester. Would you rather be named after a seaplane or a town in Tennessee?"

The joking and kidding wore thin in a few days and finally ceased as we prepared for other "battles."

The rest of Tennessee Maneuvers went smoothly and uneventfully for our crew. During May and June, the lieutenant, seeing me as a real foul ball, hardly spoke to me except in line of duty.

In late June, Tennessee Maneuvers ended. On July 1st we shipped out to Pine Camp in upstate New York, where our division became reorganized and the lieutenant left our outfit. I was still a so-called "Technician" 5th Grade, though probably not a highly respected one.

JOE

It was a lazy Saturday summery morning, a time when most of the men on our military post in upstate New York were off-duty, looking forward to a weekend of pleasure, whether relaxing in camp or going out on pass. We had come to Pine Camp almost a month earlier, following the conclusion of Tennessee Maneuvers, and during that month, in my free hours, I'd managed to dispose of much of my earnings shooting craps. Now, almost broke and disgusted with my wasteful ways, I decided to seek more healthful pleasures in town.

Standing outside the Company Orderly Room scanning the bulletin board, I saw that my request for a twelve hour, noon to midnight pass had been granted. It was to be my first pass since coming to Pine Camp.

I entered the orderly room and stopped at the first sergeant's desk.

"Yes, your pass is here," Sergeant Sands, the top-kick said, looking through a handful of passes lying on his desk. "But before you take off for town, you are to move your belongings over to the third platoon's barracks. You've been transferred to Sergeant Verhagen's tank."

"Yes, I know," I replied, "I saw my new assignment on the bulletin board when I was looking for the pass list. It's sure gonna' be tough on the second platoon losing a man like me."

"Yeah, real tough," the top-kick mumbled.

Walking into the first floor of the third platoon barracks, I saw only one man about. He was Staff Sergeant Joe Verhagen, the platoon sergeant, my new tank commander. He was sitting on the bare mattress of an unmade bunk that was located half-way down one side wall of the barracks room. All the other beds in the barracks were made up white, but the bed the sergeant was sitting on was bare, because it's new occupant was to put on fresh linen, before he left for town.

"Get off'a my bed, Sergeant!" I yelled.

"Well, if it ain't my new gunner," Joe said, disregarding my greeting. "I've just been sitting here thinking how lucky I am to have you for my gunner." Then, shaking his head as if in misery, "When I get to thinkin' that maybe you could've been assigned to me as a radio tender, I get to feelin' sick all over."

I eyed Joe strongly and raised my fist threateningly.

Again, disregarding me, my new tank commander said, "I just want to know one thing. Is it true what they say about you, that when your tank was passing by that movie theater in Manchester you poked your head through the turret and asked the lieutenant what was on at the movies?"

"How'd you like me to mash you right in your teeth!?" I asked.

Joe laughed, "Don't let nothin' but fear stop you."

Unable to top his clever response, I stood speechless for a moment.

Getting up from my bed, Joe went on. "Look, go to town and have a good time and please get drunk. For you that would be an improvement!"

Easygoing, quick-witted Joe Verhagen was a solidly built handsome six-footer, who, along with his amiable ways, possessed exceptional mechanical ability and outstanding leadership qualities. The Army, aware of his capabilities, had assigned him, in March of '42, to be part of the cadre that was sent to Camp Cooke to train and shape the 5th Armored Division which was in its formative stage.

At that time, I was a rookie in basic training and Sergeant Verhagen, as I knew him, was one of my instructors. After basic training was completed, most conversational communication between the enlisted men was carried on informally, and privates and non-coms alike called each other by first or last name only. Now he was Joe.

Rank still meant authority and responsibility, but referral by rank was reserved for commissioned officers. Non-commissioned officers were addressed by rank only when formality required it.

On that day in the summer of '43 when I was transferred to Joe's tank, I couldn't have been happier. Not only was I now a gunner, which I'd wanted to be since my first day in a tank, but I had for my commander a man I regarded as the best platoon sergeant in the whole U.S. Army.

It didn't take but a few trips to the gunnery range to prove to Joe that he'd gotten in me one of the best gunners he'd ever seen either. "I don't ever want to go into battle without you as my gunner," he told me on more than one occasion.

It was out on field problems that I got to learn a bit about Joe's background. I remember one night when we were out on bivouac and our crew was sitting around telling stories out of their past that I heard Joe's best. Joe told an amusing story of a little trouble he'd encountered as a young boy growing up on a farm back home in Kaukauna, Wisconsin. "Did I ever tell you how I got my first black eye?" he asked.

"There was this other little guy and me, both of us about eight years old, walkin' down this lonely country back road, when all of a sudden four or five bigger boys stepped out from behind some trees and started having words with my little friend. And I really didn't have time to realize that these kids meant business. Anyhow, all I know is my friend turns to me real quick, saying, 'I can whip'em, can't we?' And that's how I got my first black eye."

After hearing that, our crew's motto was "I can whip'em, can't we?"

THE CAPTAIN'S DICHOTOMY

While stationed at Pine Camp, all of us knew that our days stateside were drawing to a close. When addressing us during company assembly, Captain Pool would say quite frequently that a second front was likely in the coming year and we'd be part of it.

As good soldiers we liked to hear this, for we were all looking forward to doing our part in helping to rid the world of the Devil.

On one memorable occasion, before being dismissed following Retreat, Captain Pool had a few words to say to us regarding a new liberal pass policy that was to take effect immediately for our entire division. Reading from a memo that the general had sent out to all the company commanders, the captain said that pass restrictions were being eased considerably and nearly all men putting in for passes to town would be granted them. After informing us of the wonderful pass situation at this post, the captain added, "God knows when we're overseas passes are going to be scarce as hen's teeth, so let's all put in for passes while they're available. Remember what our forefathers intended for us to do, let's pursue happiness."

A wave of applause swept through the ranks and the captain continued.

"Now, before we go to town, there are some rules and restrictions we must all abide by. First off is this: at the time you pick up your pass at the First Sergeant's or company clerk's desk, you will be issued a pack of rubbers which you are required to take with you to town. Now I know that some of you may protest this and say that when you entered the Army you were studying to become a priest or minister or rabbi. I got no time for that bologna. I only know that this is an order! Nobody goes to town without a pack of rubbers." (I don't recall if anyone asked about the chaplains, but I supposed if they went to town they, like everyone else, had to show their package of rubbers.)

"Now about these passes," the captain went on. "All passes allow you to go into Watertown only (the town closest to our base). All passes Monday through Friday being at 1800 hours, following Retreat. Passes issued to single men end at 2400 hours, midnight. Passes for married men with wives living in town were to end at 0600 hours the following morning. Only married men with wife living in town may get an overnight pass. Saturday and Sunday passes will begin six hours earlier at 1200 hours, with ending time on pass same as those issued on weekdays. Now pay particular attention to this: Watertown has a midnight curfew. No solder, married or single, is to be on the street after midnight. MP's will pick up anyone seen violating the curfew. Another thing, all hotels are off-limits. They will accommodate no G.I.'s on six hour passes. In certain circumstances, married men and their wives can be accommodated.

"Now understand this, all you single men. Your passes tonight are good for six hours only; is that understood?"

The guy standing next to me in ranks muttered, "That don't give us too much time to use those rubbers, does it?"

"Now the last thing I'm going to talk to you about is sexual conduct and responsibility. And here I want to say that my remarks are intended for all you single men which make up over ninety percent of us, and this is what I have to say to you: Remember that you have girlfriends back home, young ladies who are looking forward to the day you honorable men return home to them, clean and wholesome as the day you entered the service. And I know you would not want to do anything that would harm your future relationships with them. Think about that!"

"All of you can recall, I'm sure, seeing your first G.I. movies about sex, you know, the ones showing people who had contacted syphilis and were in various states of falling apart and dying. These films were shown to you to make you aware of the need for social hygiene. The Army knows that despite all talking and showing of movies, sexual activity is a fact of life. And the Army feels that not only should you be well informed about these matters as they relate to your well-being, but you must also be protected, just in case. So you can understand the reason for the order on rubbers. Before leaving this subject I want to again remind you single men to think of your girlfriend who is waiting for you back home."

About this time some grumbling was heard throughout the ranks and the captain, sensing that some of his remarks were missing the target, decided he'd conclude his little talk by telling us about a very special British soldier he'd known in Tunisia. "I want you to know that this man was the fightenest man you could ever see anywhere in the world. Anyway, one day I ran across him back at the medics. He was lying on the ground, shot in both legs, unable to move. Showing no pain, he was asked by one of the medics what was the secret of his great moral strength, what lay behind his fighting spirit? Without hesitation, this brave and gallant man looked up at this medic and said, "I'll tell you in a few words, any Army that don't – don't fight!"

With these words the captain concluded his dichotomy and we were dismissed.

Later, after mulling over what I'd heard them say, I decided to go to town in quest of romance so I might become a better soldier.

THE QUEST

She was a gorgeous looking brunette, tall and quite shapely. And as I stared at her she stared back. We were in a dance hall; at a dance given by the Elk or Lions or some such civic organization that sought to provide good, clean, wholesome fun for servicemen on pass in Watertown. After we started dancing, I told her that she had a pretty mean stare. She replied that if I hadn't come over to her right at the time I did and ask her for a dance, she was going to come over and hit me on the head with her purse!

After the dance, I took her home and she invited me in for a nightcap. She lived alone as a boarder in the back room on the second floor of a large two-story house. Her room had a bed, a couch, and a radio, in addition to a kitchen.

The nightcap made us feel friendly. On the couch we fell into a clinch of delightful necking. While so engaged, time passed all too fast. I glanced once at my watch. It was 11:30. "My God!" I bolted upright. "I've only got a half hour to get to the bus station." Immediately, I fell to bemoaning my fate. "Why, oh why, do things like this always happen to me?" I cried.

"Shut up and kiss me, you fool," she whispered in a sexy voice, and playfully she pushed me back down on the couch. And so we kissed some more.

A few minutes of passionate kissing were all I had time for. By now, it was seventeen minutes to twelve. Knowing that if I screwed up by being caught out on the street after midnight, I would be dead as a door nail as far as future passes were concerned; I broke free from her embrace. Hurriedly I explained the 6-hour, 12-hour pass situation to her. "Only married men whose wives live in town can get the overnight passes which are good for 12 hours."

"Well, that seems unfair," she said.

"Well, that's the way it is," I said. "Only the guys who have a place to stay overnight, so they're not out on the streets between the hours of midnight and 5 a.m. in the morning, are allowed overnights."

"What about a hotel? What about the Woodruff Hotel? Couldn't you stay there?"

"All off-limits to us single guys," I said. "Listen, if it were possible for me to sleep here in town, I would; believe me, honey."

"Well, what about my couch? Is that off-limits, too?"

"You mean....?"

"Yes, I mean for the future. If you were able to have a place to sleep like on my couch, could you then get an overnight pass?"

"Oh, that's a splendid idea. I'll talk to the first sergeant about this kind of offer, and I'll bet he'll arrange for me to get the overnight. Yeah, I'm sure he'll do it quietly for me because he's a friend of mine."

A couple of nights later, as our company stood on the drill field waiting to be dismissed from Retreat, the booming voice of Sergeant Sands could be heard carrying throughout the entire field, "Married men and Norber get your overnight passes!"

Shock swept through the ranks of our assembled company. I, the spit-and-polish, morally squeaky clean solder who neither smoked nor drank, now stood exposed for what I really was: A sinner.

At the command, "Dismissed," one of my erstwhile buddies came up to me and said, "And to think I even wanted to take you home with me on furlough to meet my sister! You, of all people!"

No words of mine could explain to my buddies that I wasn't yet living in sin.

As soon as I got off the bus in Watertown, I phoned my girlfriend and told her the good news.

"OVERNIGHT...ALL RIGHT!" she exclaimed. "Hurry over, Lover. I'm waiting for you."

With every good intention of living in sin, I hastened to her side.

She met me at the front door of the boarding house and led me up the stairway to her room. After closing the door, she slipped into my arms and we kissed playfully. We slowly made our way to her couch, where we resumed our necking. She reached over to a small table and snapped on the radio. Romantic dance music was playing.

We got up, danced a bit, and cooled down. It was early.

"Would you care for drink?" she asked.

I really didn't want a drink, but thinking it was socially proper, I said, "Good idea."

She took me into her kitchen. On the sink were a couple of bottles of liquor. "What's your choice, "general?" she asked, promoting me a few grades.

"I'll have some of the bourbon," I said, mispronouncing what I was reading on the label.

She gave me a strange look. "That is pronounced bourbon," she said, "you know, like b-u-r."

"Just kidding," I laughed. *Any idiot knows Bourbon whiskey is not pronounced like the name of a Bourbon king, but damn it, I'd never read aloud from a whiskey bottle before. It just slipped out wrong.*

On returning to the bedroom with drinks in hand, we sat for a while on the couch sipping and smooching. At times our glasses would require refilling, so we would take a break and go back into the kitchen and get more Scotch or Bourbon or whatever else was in bottles. And so we passed the evening.

As midnight approached, we were lying together stretched out on the couch again, passionately necking and petting. On the radio soft romantic music was playing.

In the pre-dawn hours of early morning I awoke, and found her standing over me. I was sleeping on the couch and she was gently awakening me. "Get up, my darling. It's time to go back to camp."

"What happened to me?" I demanded to know. "What happened to me?"

"You passed out cold, Lover. You just plain couldn't hold your liquor."

Going back to camp on the bus, I realized that no one would believe me if I said I hadn't lived in sin. Of course, I'd say nothing to anyone anyhow, for I wasn't a loudmouth like the top-kick, and thinking of the top-kick, if he knew of my inability to handle my liquor, I'd be proclaimed a disgrace to the entire 10th Tank Battalion.

For a day or two after my first overnight, I didn't get to go back to town because we went into the field on Army business. Bivouac. On our return to the barracks, I ran into the orderly room to find out if I could go to town.

"Your overnight pass is automatic, just like the married men's are. You put in for it, you got it," the first sergeant, in charge of the orderly room said.

"Which reminds me, sergeant, don't you remember that I asked you in strictest confidence if it would be possible for me to get an overnight pass LIKE the ones the married men get? And I asked you to please handle this in a sorta' quiet manner, you know, be discreet?"

"Oh, I forgot," he said.

Shooting out of the orderly room I headed for the barracks and a good hot shower. After luxuriating in a hot shower for several minutes, I turned the shower handle to COLD and let the splash of ice cold water on my face and body invigorate me from head to foot, thus preparing me for my evening's hoped for performance.

At Retreat I stood in the cool late September evening with my wet hair neatly combed, pores closed from the cold shower, and skin smelling good from Old Spice. In my pocket was the unopened package of rubbers left over from my previous pass, and also a package of Sen-Sen, which I used for breath sweetener. I was prepared.

Following the word "Dismissed," First Sergeant Sands, with his usual dead-pan look, called out, "Married men and Norber get your overnight passes." So much for discretion!

On the Watertown bus on the way to my girlfriend's abode, I sat preoccupied with the most wonderful, pleasurable thoughts a man could possibly entertain. And even though my heart was not pure, I felt my strength was as "the strength of ten."

She met me at the door and whisked me up to her room. Scarcely had her bedroom door been closed than we found ourselves seated on her couch playfully kissing. After enjoying a bit of smooching, we poured ourselves a few drinks, and we resumed kissing and petting. Before long, she was smothering me in kisses, passionate kisses, and I heard her say, "I love you," and I just knew what was in store, and I guess, the lights went out.

From flat on my back on her couch I saw her standing above me. "It's time to get up," she said. "You've just got time to catch the bus back to camp." With sweetness in her voice, "You're a great necker, honey, but you sure can't drink worth a damned!" My second "overnight" had been a disgusting replica of my first.

Back at camp I stood Reveille and was greeted with just the news I liked to hear. We were going on a dismounted five-mile road march with full field pack.

Normally, to me it was simply a nice hike through the countryside, in which hikers are occasionally asked to double-time a bit to add to the day's enjoyment. As a non-smoker accustomed to long distance running, I had always looked forward to these little outings. But on this particular day, things were different.

By the time we took our break at the halfway point, I was starting to wonder if overnight passes were worth what I was feeling. As I lay on the ground with my head resting on my field pack, my chest and throat burned, my legs felt like lead, my head ached, and my back felt like I had been carrying a field pack loaded with large stones. All in all, I didn't feel too well. Were it not for a strong sense of pride and good recuperative powers, I would never have managed to finish the march.

By the time Retreat rolled around, I was too bushed to even consider going to town, so I phoned my girlfriend and told her not to look for me a couple of nights, Army business.

A break in my schedule at this time, I figured, not only would allow me to catch up on some much needed rest, but would also allow me to make an appearance or two at some friendly crap games.

So it was a day or so later that I was on the back stairs of the first platoon's barracks, on my way to the upstairs barracks where a crap game was in progress, that I happened to overhear a sergeant telling his friends about the weird adventures of "The Milkshake Kid." Now Sergeant Postalski, who was better known as "Piss and Moan" because he liked to groan about things like Army food, the sad state of the world, and the lack of comfortable seats in Sherman tanks, also had a light and humorous side to him that completely overshadowed his gloom and doom side, and it was this latter side that had overtaken him this night as he was telling his buddies about me, "The Milkshake Kid."

"And I'm tellin' you, right hand to Jesus, when the bus driver calls out Factory Street, our nice, clean-cut milkshake kid, with cheeks all afire, gets up from his seat, pulls the cord, and gets off the bus where nobody would dare to go. He steps out alone from the bus and disappears into the weeds over six feet high of this lot in no-man's land."

Loud laughter greets Piss and Moan's remarks, and I hear one voice pipe up with, "I've hearda guys goin' over cut glass and rusty nails to get to it, but this is the first time I've ever heard of goin' through weeds over your head!"

Standing on the back stairs, out of sight, overhearing all this, I was tempted to walk into the first floor barracks and confront Piss and Moan with the truth: the weeds were definitely not six feet high, they weren't even up to my armpits. The only thing that kept me from confronting Postalski was the sound of dice rolling across the upstairs floor. I decided to continue on my way to the game.

"Shoot the twenty," I said. I was on my hands and knees, enjoying the Army's favorite pastime.

"You'll shoot nothing!" said the voice above and behind me.

At the same time, I heard the voice I felt two hands roughly lifting me from the floor. One hand was holding me by the back of my collar, choking me, while the other hand was gripping me by the seat of my pants. Suspended several inches above the floor, I gasped to my attacker, "Unhand me immediately, you ruffian, or I shall kick your posterior end on the dorsal side!!" I always spoke like this to the person I knew was holding me because I knew this person had gone to college back east and was therefore quite erudite.

"Shaddup! You're comin' to town with your buddies and beer up. You're not going to throw your money away, not when we can all have such a good time on it!"

"But I don't drink, you know I don't drink."

"Have you forgotten what happened to you in Santa Barbara when you refused to drink with your old buddies?"

Thoughts of Santa Barbara flashed through my mind and I remembered an evening when I walked through the bar of the hotel where I was staying and I happened to run across a few of my buddies seated at the bar who invited me to have a drink with them.

No, I had said, I really didn't care to drink, and besides, I was in a hurry to get to a dance. Thinking nothing of my refusal to join them for a drink, I had gone on my way.

On the following morning the phone in my hotel room rang. The caller, one of my buddies I'd seen seated at the hotel bar the previous evening, said, "Hey, Vic, how's about joining your good buddies for breakfast?"

"Good idea," I'd responded. "Where should I meet you?"

"Oh, come on up to Sullivan's room, that's room 202, and we'll go from here."

"Okay, man. I'll be right up." Hanging up the phone, I dashed upstairs to Sullivan's room.

No sooner had I gone through the door into Sullivan's room than I was jumped on from behind by three or four guys, thrown to the floor, and pinned there.

"You insulting bastard!" they were yelling at me. "Won't drink with your buddies, huh? We'll teach you!"

As I struggled to break free from these men of questionable birth who were holding me pinned to the floor, they began spilling milk from a glass into my mouth. "Pour the goddamn milk down his goddamn throat!" And the milk bubbled from my mouth, down my cheeks onto the carpet.

Really teed off at this kind of reception, I started threatening my attackers. "When I get up, I swear I'm gonna make you all wish you never messed with me! I'm gonna break all of your arms and all your legs!"

"Then we'll never let you up!"

After a few minutes of being held on the floor by my "friends," I felt it prudent to agree to a truce. So I not only retracted my threat to them, but further agreed to never refuse to drink with them in the future.

So now, remembering what happened to me in Santa Barbara, I decided I'd better join my friends for a night in Watertown.

It was much later, after we got to town that I was sitting in a tavern drinking with my buddies, when all of a sudden I happened to glance at the table next to ours, and what or who should I see, but the most gorgeous redhead I'd ever seen in my entire life. Seated at the table with her were two or three sailors and two or three other girls. All appeared to be enjoying themselves, laughing and joking with each other. They looked to be a friendly group, so I went over to their table and asked them if they'd care to invite a few lonely G.I.'s to join them. "Come on over," they replied. "The more the merrier!"

After introducing ourselves and paying for a round of drinks, my buddies and I were soon integrated into the group. The music in the jukebox was playing in the background and I, wanting to establish rapport with the beautiful redhead, asked her if she'd dance with me.

It was while we were dancing that I started feeling like I was in another world. Holding her close to me and hearing her lilting laughter at nearly everything I said made me want to establish a relationship for the future. So I asked her for her phone number.

"I'm sorry, my father doesn't allow me to go out with servicemen," she said.

"But what about these sailors you're with?" I said. "Aren't they in service?"

"Yes, but they're hometown boys on leave, and my father knows them."

"So introduce me to your father. I could pass inspection."

She smiled. Our eyes met briefly. She was delightful.

39

Too soon it was time to break up the party and head back to camp. Before leaving I took her aside and again asked her for her phone number.

She hesitated. "My father...."

"I know, I know. Your father doesn't approve of your going out with strange servicemen. But I'm not a stranger, not now. You know me."

"Wait," she said. "Let me finish what I was going to say. Though I'm not allowed to date servicemen, my father approves of my going to U.S.O. types of dances, and next week your division is having a dance in your service club at Pine Camp. Your division's dance band, which is great, from what I hear, is going to be playing. My father has already given me his approval to go to this dance, so I'll tell you what. I'll meet you at the dance and we'll resume our friendship there."

A few evenings later, on the dance floor of the service club, I found my arms around the most beautiful girl in all the state of New York. We spent the entire evening dancing together and drinking soft drinks. There were no cut-ins or changes of partners.

When the band struck up the final number, "Goodnight, Sweetheart, 'Til We Meet Tomorrow," I asked her if we could meet some place in Watertown the next day. "If your father objects, tell him I'll come to your house for you. Tell him I'd like to meet him," I said.

She smiled. "That won't be necessary. I spoke to Dad about you. I overwhelmed him with my description of you, all lies, of course. After I said you were a knight in shining armor from the 5th Armored, Dad gave in to me and said he trusted my judgment."

As we stepped outside the service club into the cool night air, and were walking to the chartered bus from Watertown, I asked her for her phone number. She said nothing, but as she was about to board the bus, we shook hands. When we unclasped our hands, I found in my palm a slip of paper with her telephone number on it.

Now I had two girlfriends.

This was war-time. Romance was in the air. A full moon and empty arms were a thing of the past.

Not long after I started dating two girls, the beautiful brunette and the sweet red-haired angel, "Fateful Sunday" occurred.

In the middle of the night I was awakened from my sleep. "Wake up, Norber! Crap game in the latrine!" Sleepily, I arose from bed and entered into a brief crap game, blew all the money I had in my wallet, and went back to sleep.

A few hours later, when I got up and was getting dressed, I looked in my wallet and it hit me: "Oh my God," I said, "I'm broke!"

Not realizing that I was genetically programmed to be a wild crap shooter (my father suffered from the same ailment), I started berating myself for my inherent shortcoming. What made this loss so particularly painful to me on this morning was this was the day I was supposed to go over to the ticket office in camp and purchase my round-trip ticket to St. Louis. My furlough was coming up in a few days and the money I had blown in the crap game included not only my monthly pay, but also money I had set aside to purchase my train ticket.

The thought of calling Dad from St. Louis and explaining my predicament to him occurred to me, but the idea of having Dad cover my gambling losses didn't sit well with me. Yet in all of Dad's letters, he mentioned that he would be happy to send me any money I needed, should the need arise. Well, the need had finally arisen. Another possibility that came to mind was that I could borrow some money, get in another crap game, and win back what I had lost. Ideas of this sort came easily to me, given my inherent gambling weakness. At any rate, I had a couple of days to think how I could raise the money, so I put the problem momentarily on hold.

Of immediate importance to me was the fact that I needed to borrow some money so I could go to a movie with my beautiful brunette in the evening. This kind of money I knew I could borrow from my buddies. And if I couldn't come up with enough to have a good time, maybe we'd spend the entire evening at her place, and I'd really get to know her for the first time.

In the evening of Fateful Sunday, I sat on my girlfriend's couch telling her all the details of how I sleepwalked my way into a crap game and managed to go bankrupt. On hearing that I was broke and had no funds even for my train fare back home, she quietly left the room for a few seconds. When she came back she offered me seventy-five dollars, saying, "Here, Honey, I've had this stashed away. You take it and have a good time on your furlough."

Of course I wouldn't accept it, but I was shocked at her offering me her savings. "Why would you loan me money like this? It's all you have. How do you know I'll pay you back?"

Her reply was simple. "I love you, Honey, and I trust you. I know you."

Somewhere in the dark gray cell matter that occupies the cranial space between my ears, a light turned on and I realized that for the first time in my life a girlfriend of mine truly loved me. And at that moment all my ideas of romancing her to the limit were shot down. In refusing her kind offer of financial assistance, I assured her that I would phone home and get the money I needed from my father. "There'll be no difficulty, he'll be glad to hear from me," I told her.

This satisfied her, and as her face took on a smile, I looked into her deep brown eyes and I saw her clearly, a sweet and good girl, one for whom life had not been easy.

I guess this revelation that a girl with strong sensual yearnings could be sweet and good stood opposed to everything I'd been taught to believe in about women. Like most young men growing up in the late thirties and early forties, I'd thought that only bad and indecent girls did "it" outside marriage.

As I sat on her couch with her I didn't know why I felt so deeply ashamed of myself. I couldn't keep from desiring her or from kissing her passionately, yet deep in my heart I knew there was no way I was going to try to seduce her.

After enjoying a delightful evening of necking, I decided I should not spend the night at her place, so I gave her an early good-night kiss and headed back to camp.

As soon as I got back to camp I called Dad collect. He was happy to hear from me, as I knew he would be. He said he'd wire me money for my ticket and furlough in the morning.

A few days later I was back home in St. Louis, hugging and kissing my father for having redeemed me from suffering the consequences of my evil crap-shooting ways. On hearing of my weakness and lack of talent with the dice, my father consoled me with, "Don't worry my son. It's all a part of life." Such understanding puzzled me because at this time I had no knowledge of Dad's own experiences in gambling.

After visiting with my dad at my aunt's house, where he lived, I went to my cousins with whom I'd lived prior to my entering service. Here, my cousins welcomed me warmly and were more than happy to open their home to me for my two week leave. Unlike my pre-service days, I was not allowed to contribute anything to the household for my upkeep. My furlough would be a glorious free ride.

When I enlisted in the Army in March of '42, my main problems were no money and no girls. Now eighteen months later, neither of these

45

problems were present. Money I had, and the uniform I wore attracted the girls. Given my good circumstances, I was soon caught up in a whirlwind of social activity. Girls I had known previously who'd found me less than dashing, now found me romantic and were glad to go out with me. I made new friends. It seemed I was dancing and dining at The Chase Club every other night. But even as I was caught up in this playboy world, there was a vacuum in me. Something was missing. I couldn't get the red-haired beauty back in Watertown out of my mind.

On an evening two or three days before my leave in St. Louis was to have ended, I was at my aunt's house for a family get-together and dinner. At the conclusion of the meal I informed everyone that I had decided to take the morning train back east.

On hearing that I was cutting short my furlough time in St. Louis to return to the east, my folks were surprised and obviously dismayed. "You've decided to return to New York early? Why? What's wrong? You've several days left to your furlough."

So I told them about the girl I loved.

Since Watertown itself was now off-limits to me insofar as overnight passes went, I had a little planning to do. I had to figure out how I could see my honey for the remaining two or three days of my furlough without staying in Watertown overnight or returning to camp. I decided that this could best be accomplished by setting up my headquarters in Syracuse, New York, and commuting from there to and from Watertown.

No sooner had I arrived at the train station in Syracuse, than I was on my way to the Dome Hotel where I got a room. Once settled in my room, I phoned the bus station and got the schedule for buses going to and coming in from Watertown. This accomplished, I phoned by beloved, told her where I was, and asked if she'd consider going out with me according to the bus schedule.

"Just tell me the bus schedule, and see how quickly you can get here." She sounded excited.

Sitting in a restaurant booth in Watertown, gazing into the eyes of my beloved over a hamburger and chocolate milkshake, watching her sweet lips mouth sweet nothings and hearing her laugh at my jokes, "Don't laugh at my jokes too much, people will say we're in love," I sang to her from "Oklahoma."

Later, while dancing and dining at a little night club, I again sang this sweet love song to my sweetheart. I felt as though the song were written for us. It was our song.

Being in love with this girl meant I would have to break off my relationship with the dark-haired girl who had cared a lot for me. Never before had I been the one to break off a relationship, and I didn't look forward to telling her that I wouldn't be seeing her again; that I'd found somebody else. Could I lie and say it was a girl back home whom I'd resumed dating on my furlough? I didn't know. All I knew was I had to call her.

I don't remember very much of the phone call. I only remember her asking me why I was suddenly breaking off our relationship, and I remember my telling her I'd fallen in love at first sight with someone else. I told her I'd always remember the wonderful and delightful times we'd shared together (we'd never been sexually intimate), and I said had I not fallen seriously in love with someone else, things might have been different for us.

She was upset, but understanding.

When I hung up I was sad. I knew I'd done the right thing, but I felt sad knowing that I'd hurt someone who really cared for me, however short our relationship.

Within a few days I was focusing all my romantic attentions on my one true love. Besides singing to her I also took to reciting poetry to her.

Yet despite my intense feelings for her, always in the back of my mind I knew marriage was out of the question. There was a war going on and soon I'd be going overseas. Perhaps when the war was over I'd return.

My courtship of my red-haired sweetheart ran the same course that most wartime romances took. We lived for the moment, enjoying each other as other young lovers did, with our relationship never going beyond the limits of propriety. Although we kissed passionately, our morals were strictly Victorian.

On one particularly rare occasion when we were sitting on her living room couch wrapped in each other's arms and passionately kissing, passion almost overcame my sensibilities and I could feel that I was about to lose my self-control. Remembering what I'd always heard was effective in these situations; I deliberately began thinking of playing golf shots and naming pitchers on the St. Louis Cardinals. When neither of these things worked, I casually arose from the couch, walked over to the mantle-piece, and started talking about Abraham Lincoln and how he saved the Union. I veered to his famous speech. By the time I was halfway through the Gettysburg Address my ardor had cooled and I had regained complete control of myself. That, as I will always remember, was the closest I came to overstepping the bounds of propriety.

Though I, myself was not a virgin, I knew that my beloved was a Sunday School teaching virgin. And had I even made an attempt to deflower this young maiden, my contempt for myself would have been unbearable.

As the days of the 5th Armored Division's stay at Pine Camp were drawing to a close, I realized that I would soon be going overseas. We would be separated. Could I ask her not to "go walkin' down lover's lane with anyone else but me?" The answer to that had to be no. Not only was I not ready for a commitment, but she was quite young, not yet twenty. She deserved her freedom at least until someone would make the marriage vow. Our parting had to be a no-strings attached parting.

"We'll write," we promised each other as we parted on a cold night in early December '43. And we kissed and said goodbye.

ENGLAND

March 1944: When we arrived in England a month before (in late February), we were billeted in barracks just outside the city of Swindon, which is located 78 miles west of London. At the time of our arrival, all of the men in our division knew exactly what our role in the war was to be. We were to be part of the front line forces that would fight Germany on the Western Front. We were the ones who were chosen to free Europe from the grasp of the Devil. We knew that would be no easy task. Knowing this, most of us felt that our stay in England would be brief and whatever happiness we could find before battle, we'd better grab.

In our first month in England, the only passes issued to us were class A passes (6 hours). No other passes had been made available. So it was with great enthusiasm that the troops greeted the announcement that some three-day passes would be made available to the men in our division. Our enthusiasm, however, was dampened a great deal when it was learned that only two men in each platoon would be issued such passes. Who the lucky two men were was to be determined by a raffle. Each company in our command would conduct its own drawing.

On the day of the drawing, each platoon would walk single file into the company day room where each man would be issued one raffle ticket. It was a number raffle, not a name. The winners would be called out by number and not name.

After all the raffle tickets were deposited in an empty box, a company officer dipped his hand into the box and withdrew two tickets. Glancing into his hand, the officer called out, "And the winning numbers are..."

Looking at my stub, I saw that my number hadn't been called. How could it be, I wondered, that I, an Anglophile of the highest order, should be denied the privilege of visiting London, the very heart and soul of English culture? How could it be that at this very moment when every cell in my sensually deprived body cried out so desperately for female companionship? Oh, well, for the moment, at last, it appeared that another of life's little disappointments had come my way.

But wait.

As I started to leave the day-room, Joe Verhagen, who had been standing a few feet away from me, called me aside. "So you got lucky and got a three-day pass to London. I always knew you were lucky."

"Yeah, real lucky. My number wasn't even close."

"Well, what about this one?" Joe said, and he showed me his number.

"Oh, great, man, great!" I responded, happy for him that he had won. If I couldn't win there was no one else I'd rather see winning than Joe.

Handing me his winning ticket, Joe said, "Here, it's yours. You're going to London."

"Like hell I am," I replied. "You won it, man. It's yours. Now don't start that!!"

"Shut up!' Joe said. "You're going to London because I say you're going to London and I'm your tank commander and your platoon sergeant and what I say goes!"

"I'm not going to London on *your* pass. You oughta think of yourself some time. There's no way I'm going to let you give me your pass. I'm not going to take it!!"

"Okay, then, forget it," he said. "I'll give this pass to John."

Glancing over to the far side of the room, Joe called out to another member of our crew. "Hey, John, when you got a minute would you come over here for a second. I want to talk to you about something."

John, who was talking with some other members of our platoon, signaled Joe, saying "I'll be there in a minute."

Alarmed that Joe was really going to give his ticket away, give it to John, I quickly changed my mind. "Good God, Joe, don't do that. Don't give it away. I'll take it!"

"Do you give me your word you're not going to give me any more trouble about this?"

"You got it!"

Satisfied with my word, Joe said, "If I want to go to town I'll got to Swindon. Swindon's fine for me. I'm not interested in going to London." He said this, of course, so I wouldn't feel guilty in taking his pass.

John came up to Joe, saying, "What do you want to talk to me about?"

And Joe, turning from me, talked to John about something totally unrelated to passes.

Joe had easily faked me out. And he had done so in a style that was distinctly his own.

FROM NORMANDY TO THE GERMAN FRONTIER

On August 11, 1944, the lead tank of a column of tanks proceeding down a highway in Northern France was hit by an eighty-eight knocking out the tank and disabling its commander. The column momentarily halted. Sizing up the situation, the platoon sergeant commanding the number four tank, immediately took charge of the platoon, deploying it into a wooded area off the side of the highway, and took the enemy under fire. Staff Sergeant Joe Verhagen at this point became the de facto lieutenant, the new platoon leader of the third platoon.

Three weeks later, while our company was enjoying an evening meal in a little clearing in the historic Compeigne Forest, Joe said to me in a low voice, "Very casually, without any sudden movement, look to your left and see who the captain is dining with tonight."

Pausing for a moment and looking up from my food, I casually glanced to my left. Seated at a park table some thirty feet away sat the two of them dining together. The captain and the general.

I wondered what brought the general to our area that evening. The cuisine in our kitchen served was good, but great it wasn't. Obviously the general had come to our area because he wanted to confer with the captain. My suspicions were aroused about what the two of them were talking about because I noticed that both men appeared rather grim and it appeared that although they had very little to say to each other, whatever it was they spoke of must have been a very serious nature.

A few days later Joe told me that he had it on good authority that the general's son had been reported mission in action. Later I heard that son was a pilot who had been shot down over enemy lines, and later still I heard that the son had made it back to our lines. Whether or not these rumors were true, I don't know, but one thing I suspected was true was that the general had more trust in his former aide than is normal for a general to have in a company commander.

Shortly after leaving the Compeigne Forest, our division plunged through Belgium and Luxembourg and arrived at the German frontier on September 11. Here our division halted and began fanning out and setting up observation posts in the mountainous terrain of Luxembourg overlooking the Siegfried Line.

While this was going on, a patrol of foot soldiers consisting of five members of a reconnaissance patrol from CC B (Combat Command B) of the 5th Armored accompanied by a French Army lieutenant crossed the border and entered Germany, near the German village of Stalzemburg.

This entrance marked the first time since Napoleon that enemy foot soldiers, in a time of war, had invaded the soil of Germany.

The time for sound thinking and bold action had arrived. Germany was to be invaded and the battle for the Rhine was to begin.

WALLENDORF

September 12, 1944, was a clear day and as I was standing high up in the mountainous terrain looking down on a scattering of pillboxes that dotted the grassy green area of the Siegfried Line far below, I heard one of our tanks coming up the mountainside. The commander of the approaching tank, Captain Pool, leaned over the side of his turret and called out to my tank commander, "Sergeant Verhagen, mount up!.. one section (two tanks). We're going to take a reading on those pillboxes. Let's not keep the general waiting!"

Hurriedly, Joe gave orders to the last tank in our platoon to mount up. Minutes later our three tanks plus the general, in his open-air peep (jeep), were reconnoitering the pillboxes and surrounding area of the Siegfried Line. Taking target practice on the pillboxes, we soon discovered the pillboxes were unmanned. From my view, which was seen mainly through the periscope sight in my tank, all I saw was a steady stream of my shells bouncing off these concrete blockhouses. No enemy response was forthcoming, so we knew no enemy was around. After taking target practice, we milled around in the area for a while and as we maneuvered around in our tanks, I asked Joe what was going on. In so many words Joe let me know that we were thoroughly reconnoitering the area until the general was satisfied he had gotten all the information he wanted firsthand as to the lay of the land and possible places for German entrapment should our forces enter Germany here.

About an hour later, the general, satisfied with the reports received about this area, ordered our patrol back to our base in Luxembourg.

While we had been probing the Wallendorf area of the Siegfried Line on September 12, other patrols of the 5th Armored Division had been checking other areas of the Siegfried Line in our sector. It appeared that the Germans were starting to systematically man the pillboxes in those sections. Although I knew nothing of these other probes, our general, who was in charge of the overall operation, determined that Wallendorf was the weakest and least protected area in our sector of the Siegfried Line. When our division was ordered by the V Corps Commander to make a major thrust into Germany, the site for the invasion was Wallendorf.

At 1100 hours in the morning of September 14, 1944, CC R (Combat Command R) 5th Armored Division plus the 28th Division's 112th Infantry Regimental Combat Team, composed of 1st Battalion, 400th Artillery Battalion, and one battery of 987th Artillery Battalion, started moving toward the Our River, which separates Luxembourg from Germany. It's immediate objective was to establish a bridgehead on the

German side of the Our River at Wallendorf. Its mission was to capture the high ground south of Mettendorf, a village five and a half miles inside the German border.

Thirty-six hours after crossing the Our River, CC R and its attached units had swept Wallendorf clean of the enemy and was completely through the line of pillboxes in this area. Everything had gone according to plan. During the night of September 15, however, word was received at CC R's command post that enemy patrols were slipping back into Wallendorf. This plus a report that other enemy troops were threatening to cut off our command from the rear caused some uneasiness in our command's headquarters.

Until now, our command had had an easy time gaining control of the road and advancing six miles deep into Germany, but considering that we were a relatively small task force, we needed help in securing our position. This being the case, CC B was ordered into the bridgehead to assist us. Its mission was to clean out enemy troops threatening to cut off CC R from the rear and widen the base of the bridgehead.

In the afternoon of September 16, CC B moved into the bridgehead area. The Germans responded by sending additional tanks and artillery into the area. With the arrival of these reinforcements activity in the area greatly increased. Now, screaming artillery shells began bursting in all sectors of both American combat commands. Although bothersome at times, these attacks, at least on my platoon's area, were never heavy. Consequently, when the evening of September 18 rolled around, a good deal of the talk among some of the men was about getting to the Rhine and how long it would be before Germany surrendered.

In the early evening of the 18th, a day which had been relatively calm, our tank received a new loader, George B. George was replacing our regular loader who in turn had been shifted to another tank crew in our company. At the time of George's arrival, our platoon was at the base of a huge well-forested hill. We were stuck in open country and were clearly visible to friend and foe alike. Ahead of us about two hundred yards away, there appeared a gentle rise in the ground and beyond the rise was a wide expanse of open undulating ground. This was tank country.

Behind us in the well-forested region near the top of the hill overlooking our area, sat the rest of our company, well concealed and well prepared to meet any challenge from German tanks, should they attempt to attack us in open tank country.

Feeling that George would probably like to survey our immediate area, I asked him if he would care to leave our tank and take a walk with me for a look-see.

As we walked toward the rise overlooking the rolling plains, I was well aware of George's reputation of being an outstanding brawler. As to his scrappy nature, I didn't have to look any further back than to this most recent encounter with the Germans. In this encounter, George had found himself in a disabled tank rolling out of control. Its tracks broken by 88 fire, the tank was ordered abandoned. Hastily getting over to the gunner's side of the turret and about to make a quick exit, George had a thought which delayed him. He decided it would be smart to blind the Germans by firing a white phosphorus (smoke) shell. He quickly slammed a shell into the breech of the cannon and fired. A split second later a German shell came crashing into the turret. Fortunately for George, at the precise moment it exploded he was standing directly under the turret opening. Instead of splattering him against the walls of the turret, the force of the explosion sent him flying upwards in an arc high above his disabled tank. On his downward descent towards earth, he appeared to be falling into a blazing haystack.

According to his buddies from whom I heard this story, it appeared that George had fallen into the middle of the burning haystack, disappearing entirely from view for a second or two. But then, as his buddies stared in horror, George emerged from the haystack and was seen running as quick as a bolt of lightning to the rear.

In reality, George missed the burning haystack by a good two or three feet and was completely unharmed. Racing through a hail of machine gun bullets, he made his way to a less perilous zone occupied by friendly troops.

Captain Pool, knowing what happened, decided George ought to get a break from fighting, so he arranged for transportation to take him to a nearby rest area. However, George, refusing to believe he needed a rest, ditched his transport, and made his way to our company in the bridgehead area. Suddenly, reappearing before Captain Pool's tank, he demanded reassignment to another tank in our company.

Obligingly, Captain Pool sent him to Joe's tank (our tank.)

Now, George and I stood talking at the crest of the hill overlooking the wide-open spaces before us. Knowing of George's scrappy nature, I decided to say something to tell him I was a tough guy, too. Extending my right arm forward and pointing my index finger northwesterly at the open terrain that lay spread out below and before us, I said, "Take a good look at those plains, Georgie. Great tank country, eh?" Waiting for this to sink into his imagination, I added, "I'm hoping that tomorrow we'll see those plains flooded with German tanks!"

Responding to this, George said, "I wish you wouldn't talk like that. So-and-so said the same thing just before my last battle and it happened."

Sensing that George's nerves were frayed, I quickly explained to him that I was no more looking forward to seeing a lot of German tanks out there than he was.

Accepting my explanation, George said, "I still wish you hadn't said that."

And the matter was dropped.

On the following morning, before a decent breakfast hour, I was standing alongside our tank heating a can of meat and beans in my skillet. I was planning to dine alone because nobody on our outpost at the base of the big hill had arisen. Some of our infantry positioned nearby would warn us if the enemy appeared, so I was feeling quite secure as I went about making myself a good, hot breakfast.

While alongside my tank cooking breakfast, I happened to glance toward the ridge on which George and I had talked the previous evening. *Good God, what I saw on the middle of the ridge!*

A German tank was pointing its gun barrel right down my throat. On each side of it, slightly to the rear and almost out of sight, more tanks appeared in wedge formation.

In a state of alarm, I jumped into the tank turret and grabbing the mike, radioed Captain Pool. No sooner had Captain Pool answered than I blurted, "German tanks right in front of us!"

Captain Pool, trying to calm me down, said, "Take it easy, Norber. We're expecting some new tanks up here to help us. Pershings, can you see their tracks?"

Adjusting the field glasses I had grabbed in the turret, I tried to make out the tracks. But the tracks were in defilade, obscured from my vision, because the German tanks were situated on the reverse slope of the ridge. "Can't see the tracks, in defilade." Now staring at the German commanding the lead tank, I saw him extending his arms, signaling. Why he was signaling his troops rather than radioing them I don't know, but for a second, he held his arm high and stationary.

At this moment I heard Captain Pool radio the leader of our first platoon. "Rollins!" the captain called out excitedly. "Open fire immediately or we'll lose our 3rd platoon!" Actually, I could be slightly off-target on the exact wording after the captain said "Rollins", because at the precise moment two legs had jumped in the turret with me. It was Joe and he was yelling to our crew, "Mount up! Mount up!"

From above and behind us the hills were now alive with the sound of gunfire, music to our ears. The German tanks, without firing a shot at us, backed down the reverse slope of the ridge. They were completely hidden from our platoon's view, but not from the rest of our company's view.

Captain Pool ordered Joe to stay in place, "'Til I give the command to move out."

At the captain's direction, Joe moved our platoon into action. A beautiful sight greeted my eyes when we reached the ridge. Spread out in the wide expanse of open fields were German tanks, fleeing in disarray, their broadsides exposed to our platoon's guns. Firing rapidly, I scored several direct hits. Up and down the line, other guns were shelling the fleeing Germans. The rout was complete.

Spotting other targets and locations that posed a threat to our flank, Joe commanded our driver to move to our right towards a small, but densely wooded area.

Skirting the edges of the woods and spraying 30 caliber machine gun fire to discourage any enemy infantry fire which may be present, our tank was wheeling around the corner of some tall trees when we almost ran right into the front of a German tank. The tank had been shielded from our view by the trees. At a range of ten or fifteen feet I needed no fire order. Joe's reaction on running up against this iron monster was to shout, "Fire, Vic!" Instantly I fired. The shell bounced off. "Fire again!" Another shell bounced off. On firing the first shell, we didn't know the tank was abandoned, but now as we were bouncing three or four shells off its frontal armor we knew for sure it was. On our fourth or fifth shot, our shell went through the German tank's gun shield, exploding inside the tank turret. Immediately the shells in their ready rack went off, and as the tank belched fire from its turret, fiery debris started spewing all over our tank. Joe commanded our driver to back up. Our acceleration to the rear was probably the fastest *ever executed on the entire western front.*

Following this, our tank, accompanied by our platoon of married infantry and other tanks in our platoon, entered the wooded area searching for signs of German infantry which had accompanied their tanks. Satisfied our sector had been swept clean of the enemy, our tanks and infantry returned to our original positions at the base of the hill. The battle was over. The Germans had been completely routed.

Even before the smoke from the battle had settled, Captain Pool was on the scene making an inspection of the German equipment burning in our sector. Counting ten German tanks still burning, plus two half-tracks burning with additional vehicles burning, the captain appeared pleased.

The force located back in the hills was well prepared to rout the enemy and would have done so without our help had the leading German tank commander not hesitated when he unexpectedly came upon our exposed tank platoon.

In the afternoon of this, our fifth day in Germany, our command began receiving the heaviest shelling we had ever received up to this point in the war. The Germans, fighting on their own soil, brought up additional artillery including railway guns and blanketed our position from the base of the hill to the top of the hill with several intense artillery barrages. Although the attack was quite heavy, we were protected by our steel forts and not affected appreciably by it. We felt secure knowing that only a direct hit could kill us. When we first heard a rumor that the Germans were firing railway guns at us, the tank crews joked and kidded about the report. After one particularly close earth-shaking miss, Joe remarked he knew that the railway guns were firing at us because a caboose had just landed next to our tank.

On two or three breaks in these barrages, our platoon accompanied by our married infantry platoon made sweeps into wooded areas to search for enemy troops we suspected may still be holed up there. In each instance, our infantry expected covering fire from our tank's 30 caliber coaxially mounted machine gun. The machine gun, however, kept jamming after discharging one or two shots, so we had to resort to firing our 75mm cannon directly over their heads into the trees 50 yards ahead of them.

The jamming of our machine gun in close quarters on these necessary sweeps into the woods was wearing on George's nerves. Several times following a sweep, he detail-stripped the machine gun and reassembled it, still our co-ax machine gun would fire only once or twice and then jam. The gun was useless (later we found the barrel locking spring was fouled). The pressure on George as loader had been intense all day long, yet he had performed his duties in a cool and very capable manner.

So I was shocked when he looked over at me in the late afternoon, mumbling, "These things are burning coffins." Before I had a chance to say anything he mumbled these same words again, "These things are burning coffins." Now I looked directly at him and saw that he was trying to take the machine gun down again. As he sat fumbling with the back plate, trying to remove it, I could see his hands were trembling so badly he would not be able to strip the gun. Seeing this I poked my head through the turret and told Joe that George was fatigued. He had simply had too much battle. I knew when the peep came to our tank to take him back to the medics, I'd never see him again.

Daylight was fast fading into darkness, and as our men were becoming shadows in our position at the base of the hill, I watched two important figures in our small group discussing plans for our upcoming night-time operation.

Joe told me that our combat command had been ordered to abandon the bridgehead we'd established in Germany. We were withdrawing under cover of darkness back to the Our River and from there we would re-cross the Our and reassemble back in Luxembourg. Since our platoon and accompanying infantry platoon were separated by a mile or so from the rest of our company, plans called for us to rendezvous with them at a designated place on the map which Captain Pool had carefully selected. The infantry lieutenant, not quite certain about the location of this particular rendezvous point, had requested a conference with Joe. Even though we controlled all the road in our area, we did not control the hills and valleys surrounding us, nor the open ground behind us. Should we get lost or even momentarily stray from a safe path, our group could most certainly be cut to ribbons. Tanks, because of their restricted vision at night, lack accurate firepower and are extremely vulnerable to enemy infantrymen carrying anti-tank weapons. With this restriction, our infantry served as our eyes and preceded us in any type of night movement, whether we were moving up or withdrawing.

When the confab with the infantry lieutenant ended, Joe returned to our tank and gave our crew the scoop. "We're going to lead and they're going to follow us. Captain Pool is going to give the order when to move out and that should be some time tonight after it's good and dark. Any questions?"

There was one. "How come we're leading?"

Joe was direct. "The lieutenant is not absolutely certain about the location of the rendezvous point, and after we talked it over we decided it's best if I lead the way since I know exactly where the rendezvous point is and how to get there, no sweat."

When night fell we moved out and found our way to the link-up point unerringly. When Joe said "no sweat" we believed him because we knew how competent he was.

By 0400 hours, September 20, our entire combat command had re-crossed the Our River and was back in Luxembourg. Our incursion into Germany had met with marked success. German losses in armor and personnel had been vastly greater than ours. Yet despite our battlefield accomplishments, we had been ordered to withdraw from Germany because of logistical problems. Not only must an Army be able to supply its troops with enough ammunition and fuel to enable it to advance, but it must also be able to rotate battle-weary troops out of the lines and replace them with fresh troops. And since, according to General Gerow, our Corps Commander, these essentials were not available to us, we were ordered to withdraw from Germany.

It should be noted that General Gerow's order canceling our advance into Germany was given to General Oliver on the night of September 16, two and a half days before our tank battle occurred. At 1300 hours, September 17, Operation Market Garden, the most daring and impressive offensive strike on the entire Western Front was launched, and that operations requirements received priority over all other operations that were in progress along the German border. These facts I learned several years after the War, which ended my confusion as to why we withdrew from Germany after routing their forces.

On our return to Luxembourg, we set up camp on the outskirts of the city of Diekirch. Tarps tied to the sides of tanks and extended to posts some twelve feet from the tank served as shelter. Pup tents were the rule for infantry. It was tent city. The atmosphere was relaxed and comfortable. After the battlefield it seemed like a resort area. For a couple of days, tankers and infantrymen sat around swapping stories about things that had happened to them in battle. All of the enlisted men, tankers and infantrymen were on a first or last name only basis. Rank was never referred to, although officers, if present, were still addressed by their rank.

On our first full day in tent city I slept late, showered, shaved, and ate a C-ration breakfast that tasted as good as bacon and eggs to me. It was great to be alive.

One of the things that struck me in talking with our married infantry platoon was the high regard these men had for Joe. Every one of them from their lieutenant on down looked upon Joe as a "special". Had the decision been left to them, Joe would have received his battlefield commission then and there.

Two days after we returned to Luxembourg, we were rejoined by CC B so they too would enjoy a breathing spell. Like us, their move back to Luxembourg had been made during the night and completed at 0400 hours in the morning, so we knew how weary these troops were.

In the early afternoon following CC B's return to Luxembourg, Joe came up to our tank crew saying, "We're going back in. Something's come up that's very urgent."

Joe explained: While CC B's was evacuating the bridgehead, one truck had slipped off the road and bogged down as their column approached the river. Battle weary men operating in darkness simply couldn't extricate the truck. Harassing fire from enemy troops didn't help matters either. An on-the-spot decision was made to leave the truck where it was, just off the side of the road partially obscured from view by the foliage of nearby trees. The truck was located just across the border on the German side of the Our River.

The truck itself was unimportant, but the cargo the truck was carrying was another matter. The cargo, Joe said, included quartz crystals which were used in our frequency modulated radio sets and if these were to fall into German hands, they could gain access to our radio channels. This, being the case, the Army was dispatching a special infantry unit to us whose mission would be to retrieve these communication parts the best way possible.

Only a limited number of infantry and tanks could be used in the operation due to the narrow, tree-lined road and restrictive surrounding terrain. The officers who planned this retrieval felt a small special infantry force accompanied by a section of tanks could get the job done. Captain Pool was to provide the tanks and Joe to furnish the armored part of the assignment.

When our crew asked exactly who this infantry outfit was, Joe said he didn't know. He only knew they were definitely the best; possibly they were "being flown in for this mission." That was good enough for us.

My personal hope, probably the hope of all our crew, was that our infantry accompaniment would be Rangers. In this little briefing by Joe, I learned that while we were sleeping, our own infantry battalion had been called out during the night to help cover the withdrawal of CC B's forces, and so they were not considered for use in this mission.

Around noon or shortly thereafter, our section took up a position in a wooded area on the west bank of the Our River. In front of us was a line of trees on the river bank.

Sitting inside the tank waiting for our infantry to arrive I felt especially alert and confident. The two-day respite from battle had had a healthful effect on me physically and mentally, and now I was ready to take on anything. Our co-ax machine gun was in working order. Its faulty barrel locking spring had been replaced, and our regular loader had returned to our crew. Joe, who had never shown any sign of ever getting tired under any conditions, was his usual cheery self and all seemed right with the world to me, except of course, there was a war going on.

At different times a squad or two of friendly infantrymen would appear filtering in and out among the trees. At these times Joe would dismount from the tank and go to the squad leader to find out if they were the special infantrymen who were to hook up with us. On learning they weren't, Joe would be disappointed.

As the afternoon wore on and the daylight hours seemed to be rapidly ticking away, we were becoming a bit concerned about when our infantry would arrive. Our armor had to be employed preferably before dusk and certainly before darkness. Rangers and special infantry outfits could operate well in darkness. We could not.

Somewhere behind us from another vantage point, Captain Pool, in touch with our situation, was also becoming concerned. In the early afternoon hours he had broken radio silence at intervals of perhaps forty-five minute wanting to know our status. Now as the sun was starting to go down his terse, "Three One (third platoon lead tank), have the doughs arrived yet?" was punctuating radio silence at intervals of less than a half hour. Joe's negative responses were becoming worrisome to the captain. Courageous, aggressive and clear-minded he was, but foolhardy he was not. He was not about to waste his men.

At dusk, the captain ordered us to return to base. The mission was cancelled, at least for this day.

On the following morning Joe said our mission was scrubbed, the problem had been successfully dealt with. Whether the truck and its cargo were retrieved or whether the cargo alone was retrieved, I didn't know. All I heard was the problem had been solved.

In looking back at our cancelled mission, I thought again how highly Captain Pool must regard Joe to have chosen him for this mission that required outstanding leadership and skill.

On returning to our rest area in Diekirch, Luxembourg, we joined our buddies in peaceful activities. For about a week we enjoyed such things as walking through the town, getting our pictures taken at the local portrait studio and girl-watching.

Then we were off to a relatively quiet sector in Belgium known as the Malmedy Eupen area. And here we rotated in and out of the lines with other American troops enjoying a breather. It was easy duty, free from the strain of severe combat.

One lovely autumn afternoon our platoon was situated in the line among some trees which were on the high ground overlooking a spacious valley. We had moved up during the night and very carefully camouflaged our tanks with tree branches. Tied to the rear deck of our tank, only partially camouflaged, clearly visible to the sky overhead, was an orange panel. This colored panel identified us. It told our Air Corps that we were American Forces.

Since our Air Corps had complete control of the skies overhead, we had not a worry in the world of being spotted by the Luftwaffe.

Standing alongside our tank on this lovely day, watching a formation of fighter planes flying overhead, stood our crew. It was comforting to us to know that we had complete control of the skies. As this formation flew directly over our position, the orange panel was clearly visible to them. So we thought.

After scanning us briefly, the formation continued on its way toward the German lines. That is, all except one plane continued in formation. This lone plane peeled off from the other planes and swooped in quite low near our tank for a good look-see. No sweat. But then, as we stared in utter amazement, this P-47 turned and banked again and made a bee line directly at our tank. Seeing this, Joe and I scrambled up the tank and threw the scattering of tree branches off the rear deck, thereby more clearly revealing our American identity. The P-47 approaching us pulled up immediately and flew off to rejoin his formation.

On the back deck of our tank, Joe and I both heaved a sigh of relief. Joe remarked that if the Germans, located about a half-mile off from us, had any doubt about our tank being here, he was sure they had none now. Nevertheless, we went about our business of re-camouflaging the rear deck.

Shortly after this incident, while we were still lounging around our tank, we heard the sound of a peep approaching us from behind. Seconds later, the peep, carrying an officer and his driver, pulled up to our tank. The officer introduced himself to Joe and our crew, saying that he was Officer So-and-So. He was a psychiatrist sent to us by First Army headquarters. His mission was to observe "men under stress."

After briefly explaining to us that he intended to spend the night with us, the officer turned to his driver and told him to toss a bedroll on the ground. After that, he dismissed his driver, telling him to go somewhere in the rear. He said when he was through with his mission, he'd contact him by walkie-talkie.

As the driver drove off, Joe took the officer aside and briefly orientated him, telling him what to do in case of enemy artillery fire and so on. Following that, the officer walked over to me and engaged me in friendly conversation. This being the first time in my life I had ever gotten to have a real enlightened discussion with a personage who knew about such things as inferiority complexes, anxieties, and feelings of insecurities, I decided to take advantage of the situation by discussing a few of these things plus a few of my own.

As luck would have it, a terrible thing happened as I was barely into explaining "my insecurities" to this psychiatrist when out of nowhere four or five mortars suddenly fell near our tank. Mortars, not even having a warning whine, just a whoosh and whomp, took this officer by complete surprise. Falling back against the tank, his helmet popped off and fell to the ground. Immediately I thought he had been hit so as he bounced off the side of the tank I exclaimed, "Are you hurt, sir?"

His eyes flashed fear. A sure sign of an insecure feeling. Before waiting for another surprise of any sort, he was on his walkie-talkie talking to his peep driver. A few minutes later the peep pulled up. The officer threw his bedroll in back, and here it looked to me like he wasn't going to spend the night with us after all. So sensing that he was going to get the hell out of here, I said to him, "But, sir, you don't know how men react under stress yet."

"I know, I know," the officer shot back at me as his peep sped away with him.

Actually, I understood him very well. His training hadn't prepared him for his mission.

I didn't have to wait long for the good-natured ribbing to start. Word had spread through our platoon that I had been seen talking with a psychiatrist. And this word was followed by voices cutting through the tree-lined woods.

One voice started it. "Hey, I hear the Army sent a psychiatrist out here to check on the nuts."

And another voice replied, "Boy, he sure knew the right tank to go to."

The first voice came on again. "What happened to that psychiatrist?"

And voice two said, "I dunno; all I know is I saw him talking to Norber for a few minutes and then a couple of mortars came in and the next thing I see is that poor psychiatrist gettin' the hell out'a here."

"Too much Jerry artillery?" asked the first voice.

"Nah, too much Norber,"

While this conversation was going on for my benefit, I listened quietly, enjoying the attention I was getting.

Getting no response from me, my benefactors started up again. "They tell me that psychiatrist came from First Army."

"First Army, hell, that guy was sent by the Secretary of the whole U.S. Army in Washington, D.C. Belletiere is offering 20 to 1 that Norber could drive every psychiatrist in the U.S. Army crazy."

I had enough of this insane chatter now, so I responded. "Ha, ha, ha, what's so funny?"

The answer wasn't long in coming. "He ain't got no takers!"

I couldn't top this answer, nor did I care to. Years later I would see what remarkable intuition Belletiere had in seeing me come up against psychiatrists. There had been a substance of a sort in his remark about me facing psychiatrists. And even though Balletiere's scenario had the wrong outcome, to this very day I still think of Belletiere as having been prophetic.

By the middle of November, Joe had been our platoon leader for three months, though he still held the rank of staff sergeant. No mention was ever made of Joe's receiving a battlefield commission. All the men in our platoon just took it for granted that Joe would be our leader until a proper replacement officer was sent to our company.

And that was the problem. Rumor was afloat in our company that three or more replacement officers had been sent to Captain Pool, but he had rejected all of them, preferring to keep Joe as the third platoon leader.

In order to find out whether or not these rumors were true, I sought out Into Ylisto, the captain's tank driver. Into, the Wild Finn as he was known, was one of my best buddies, and I knew I could depend on him to tell me the score.

"Yeah, there was some lieutenants who showed up here," Into said, "and I saw a couple a' them myself. Hell, one didn't have his shoe strings tied right and another one had uneven sideburns. It was shameful. Sure the captain rejected them. I would've too. And this you can bet on. Joe's not going to be replaced as long as Captain Pool's our company commander!"

Heading back to my tank, I felt a wonderful sense of security knowing that Joe would always be our platoon leader as long as Captain Pool had the final say-so. I had become so used to peaceful type patrol duty, I seemed to forget for a time there was a war going on. That Captain Pool or Joe or any or all of us could become casualties just didn't seem to register in my mind.

It would take our first battle in the Hurtgen Forest to reawaken me to the fact that there was a war going on.

In late November, our command was given the mission to capture the village of Hurtgen in the Hurtgen Forest. On an icy cold sleety morning, November 25, our column of tanks churning over a muddy road en route to the village, became stymied by a huge crater in the road. Unable to jump the crater or make a pathway around it, our command called our engineers forward to erect a span over the crater.

Because the crater was located at a place in the road where it was surrounded by dense woods infested with Germans, the bridging operation had to be carried out under intense enemy fire. While directing the engineers, the commander in charge of the operation was wounded and had to be evacuated. Captain Pool, who had gone to the crater to assess the situation, began directing the bridging operation while standing in the turret of his tank. As he was giving instructions, he was hit by German burp gun fire. Disregarding his wounds, the captain climbed out of his tank and got to the ground to help the engineers. Now, while helping the engineers on the ground, he was again wounded, this time by mortar fire. Refusing to be evacuated, Captain Pool, weakened by loss of blood, was placed in a peep by a medic and driven to the rear for evacuation.

As the peep passed our tank in the column, I caught a glimpse of him through my periscope. He was drenched in blood and saying something loudly to the medic. I couldn't make out what he was saying, but Joe, standing in our turret, heard him say, "This is sheer suicide. They're gonna kill all my men!" Oblivious to his own pain, he thought only of his men. This was our captain.

Following the captain's departure, CCR Commander, Colonel Glen H. Anderson, seeing the battle shape up much as Captain Pool had seen it, wisely ordered our command to withdraw. And so we pulled out to another area not far away where higher echelon officers in our command began making plans for the taking of other strategic objectives in the forest. Kleinhau, Brandenberg, and Bergstein.

The command of our company now was taken over by First Lieutenant Lewis R. Rollins, a man who had brilliantly and audaciously led our first platoon in the drive across northern France and into Germany. And at Wallendorf, in the invasion of Germany, he distinguished himself by leading his platoon in the face of enemy fire up a steep narrow winding road that led into the town. Being a typical hell-for-leather, yet sensible man, his taking over as our new company commander meant we would again be led by a fine competent officer.

Though Lieutenant Rollins knew a great deal about tanks and how to maneuver them, he was unfortunately uninformed about Captain Pool's habit of rejecting all officers sent to our outfit to replace Joe as third platoon leader. And lacking this particular bit if information, our new commander allowed a replacement officer to slip into our company to replace Joe as third platoon leader.

When the news reached our platoon that some unknown First Looey had arrived in our company to replace Joe, all of us shook our heads in disbelief. How the hell, we wondered, could some unknown from a replacement depot replace such a tried and proven combat leader as Joe, whom we all knew should be a commissioned officer? How was this possible, especially just before a battle? While the men in our platoon thought about this, a meeting was called and we all got a chance to meet our new leader, First Lieutenant Jack Cullin.

The lieutenant, with two strikes on him, met each of us and spoke with us briefly about Bergstein, giving no details except to say he had already gone over some of the battle plans with Joe. He appeared to us to be a no-nonsense guy who knew what the score was. Friendly and confident, he came across to the men as a straight shooter.

After the meeting broke up, I got a chance to speak with Joe privately. I wanted to know about Bergstein and the lieutenant. In answering me, Joe carefully and candidly explained the situation to me like this:

Bergstein was not just another tiny spot on the map that was to be just another battle. No, Bergstein was the major objective in the drive through the Hurtgen Forest to the Roer River. And the V Corps, whose mission it was to Capture Bergstein, was giving this battle its best shot. For that reason only the best veteran combat officers were being sent to us by Corps for this particular battle. And, Joe added, in going over the battle plans for Bergstein, he found Lieutenant Cullin to be a very alert, aggressive, and likeable guy.

After talking with Joe, I felt we were lucky to get this fine officer as a replacement.

On the following day, five minutes before we jumped off for Bergstein, Joe said, "It's going to be a rough trip and I'm glad he's leading."

"How rough you think it'll be?" I asked.

"You just hit the prayer book," Joe said.

And though he said it in a joking manner, I suspected he really meant it. So I reached into my shirt pocket and felt my small prayer book. I always prayed before battle.

BERGSTEIN

The enemy was waiting, concealed in the forest that lay some three hundred yards beyond the crest of the hill.

It was mid-afternoon on a cold and dreary day, December 5, 1944, and our tanks and armored infantry were rolling across open ground in battle formation. As we neared the crest, I leaned forward in my tank seat, tensed for action, my eyes glued to the gunner's periscopic sight. Suddenly Joe's voice, interrupting the tension, came over the intercom commanding our driver to pull up and stop.

Behind my back and just above me in the turret some sort of commotion was going on. Glancing around for just a second, I saw Joe's legs leaving the turret and another pair of legs replacing his. I heard a new voice coming over the intercom addressing me not as "gunner," but as "Norber."

"It's me, Norber. Lieutenant Cullin. My transmitter went out. Sergeant Verhagen and I are swapping tanks. We're the lead and he'll have the last section. Driver, move out!"

Lieutenant Cullin had addressed me because he saw that I had become alarmed at the commotion that had occurred behind me, and even though he addressed me, the message was for our whole crew.

As we neared the crest, I leaned forward in my gunner's seat tensed for action. Now, as our tank nosed over the ridge of the hill I saw heading toward us a blue white streak, the tracer, trailing the shell that was going to hit us. The impact was jarring. The traversing gears around the turret ring clashed together and sparks showered the inside of the turret basket. By the driver's seat the fuel line snapped. In the assistant driver's seat the 30 caliber machine gun had been driven through its holding spindle and had come to rest in the assistant driver's lap. Above the assistant driver the overhead hatch had become sealed. But we were lucky. The shell had ricocheted and no one was hurt.

As a well-trained gunner, I traversed the turret back to the tracer line and fired.

"You got 'em, Norber, you got 'em!" shouted Lieutenant Cullin as the German anti-tank gun blew up.

With my eyes still glued to the sight I spotted in the forest line, dead ahead, the tops of some tall timbers which were swaying. I fired at the base of the swaying trees. A huge fire broke out in the forest; the blaze seemed to momentarily cover my entire periscope. A German tank flushed by the fire came barreling out of the forest, fleeing in panic, its broadside exposed, making it a perfect target.

Our tank driver, sitting by gasoline dripping from the ruptured fuel line, suddenly panicked, and threw our tank into reverse. In a matter of seconds, our tank backed from the crest until we were on the reverse slope of the hill with just the turret peering over the crest of the hill. Here we halted.

Now, with our tank tiling backward and our gun barrel correspondingly pointing upward, I saw at the very bottom of my sight a German tank fleeing from the blazing forest. It was traveling left to right, broadside fully exposed. Attempting to pick up the target, I began depressing the barrel of the gun while power traversing the turret to the right.

"Fire, Norber, fire!"

But I couldn't fire, at least not effectively. For in depressing the barrel the breech end of the gun, inside the turret, had seesawed upwards causing the breech guard to hit the top of the turret, thus preventing me from depressing the barrel far enough to bear on the target. Frustrated, I began yelling, "Move forward! Move forward!"

And while I was yelling to move forward, Lieutenant Cullin was shouting, "Fire, Norber, fire!"

In desperation I bounced around in my gunner's seat, grabbed the lieutenant's leg and pointed to the breech of the gun. Seeing the breech guard jammed up against the top of the turret, Lieutenant Cullin immediately commanded, "Driver, move forward, move forward!"

But our driver, in a state of panic, was unable to respond.

Luckily at this time, Van Arkel's tank which was nearby opened fire on the fleeing German tank, knocking it out.

Somehow our driver momentarily overcame his feelings of panic and managed to move our tank cautiously forward to an area at the crest of the hill where we held a commanding view of the battlefield and the blazing forest.

After firing a couple of rounds into the non-burning part of the forest and getting no response, it was obvious that for all practical purposes the firefight for Bergstein was over. We had won.

A jubilant Lieutenant Cullin, standing tall in our turret, was radioing our acting Company Commander, Lieutenant Rollins, that we had accomplished our mission. After making this report, the lieutenant turned to me and said he was going to check on the rest of our platoon and also was going to confer with the Platoon Leader of our accompanying armored infantrymen. Plans had to be drawn up to meet the German counter-attack, which was sure to come by the following day.

Before leaving me in charge of the tank, the lieutenant told me that if we received indirect artillery fire from German batteries located to the rear of the forest line ahead of me, I should not return fire with our cannon, but should radio our own V Corps artillery for response. If the Germans managed to get direct fire on us, I would respond with our cannon. But considering the forest ahead of us was still glowing with fire, it appeared highly unlikely that the Germans could get reinforcements into the forest at this time, so the threat of direct fire appeared quite remote. After briefing me on our situation and making sure I knew that corps artillery ended their fire order with range followed by deflection, which was the exact opposite of tank fire order, the lieutenant left our tank.

I had been standing in the turret of our tank observing the tree-lined forest that seemed to stare back at me from three hundred yards away. Dusk was starting to set in and in the twilight it seemed to me that the fire in the forest was going out. Closer in, some seventy-five yards to my left rear, stood the remains of a farmhouse; a couple of half-demolished walls standing around emptiness, under which there was a basement.

93

Before leaving our tank, the lieutenant had told me he intended to confer with the infantry platoon leader in the basement of that demolished farmhouse, so I knew where he could be reached if needed quickly.

I was alert, but my mind was idling when suddenly the hatch cover over the driver's seat popped open and I saw our driver closely followed by our assistant driver emerging through the open hatch. As they were scrambling to the ground, I thought I heard them saying something about "getting out of here." Now, standing a few feet from the tank they both stopped and yelled to me that the tank should be abandoned. Both men were obviously badly shaken. "It's gonna blow up!" yelled our driver. "You and Mac (our loader), get outta there!" I refused to join them, and presumed to answer for Mac also, saying, "No, we're staying right here." After saying goodbye to them, I turned to Mac who was seated inside the turret, and asked him if he wanted to leave. "No way," he said, "I'm staying with you."

Fortunately, our driverless tank was in good position. Although we were the point tank situated almost at the crest of the hill, we were not fully exposed to direct fire from the enemy because our tank was sitting in a slight depression in the ground and in this position our tracks were in defilade though our turret was fully exposed. I felt like we were jutting out at a point where the entire German Army was taking aim on us.

Up ahead of our tank some ten or fifteen yards running along the crest line was a long deep World War I type of trench the Germans had prepared for the defense of Bergstein. Though the trench had not been manned when we approached Bergstein, with the capture of the Bergstein Ridge, it fell into our hands. My attention was drawn to the trench because a few of our infantrymen were examining it, probably checking to make sure it wasn't booby-trapped. Anyhow, if it checked out, our infantry would benefit from the labor of the Germans.

While Mac and I were keeping watch, Lieutenant Cullin returned to the tank briefly to tell us that he had seen our drivers back at the Infantry C.P., that they were badly shaken and had to be evacuated. After saying he'd get us new drivers, he headed back to the Infantry C.P. Obviously the situation on the hill was quite demanding, but Mac and I knew Lieutenant Cullin could handle it because he had acted so coolly and competently in leading us into Bergstein.

Shortly after he left, we began receiving indirect fire from German batteries situated in the forest well behind the tree line facing us. I did not respond, for this is what the Germans would have desired so they could pin-point our gun in the dark. Instead, as previously instructed by Lieutenant Cullin, I radioed our field artillery for help. What followed was one of those classic screw-ups that sometimes occur in battle.

Before giving the fire order, I clearly stated that I would give them their fire order with range preceding deflection. The artillery fired first for effect. I gave the adjusting fire with range preceding deflection. The next round which should have landed in the forest, fell short and landed on our position. Fortunately, no infantry were up and about and I wasn't hit sitting on the tank turret so there were no casualties. Radioing the results to our artillery, I pointed out that I ended the fire order with range preceding deflection. After making certain we understood each other, we started from scratch again.

First they fired for effect and then I called the adjusted fire. And again, our tank got some of the shrapnel. That was enough for me. So I said, "Cease fire."

I decided the lieutenant should be informed of what was happening, so I hiked over to the command post to talk with him. On my way there I happened to notice that the fire near the tree line at the forest's edge had burned out (or possibly been extinguished), and I could see lights playing among the trees and hear the sounds of the enemy digging in. For the Germans to do this before our faces meant either they didn't know of our presence on the hill or else they didn't care.

On hearing what had occurred with our artillery and seeing the Germans starting to dig in, Lieutenant Cullin decided to return to our tank where he would personally take charge in commanding our artillery to fire on the enemy.

I was sitting on the turret ring with the lieutenant while he ordered the firing. On his first adjustment he got the same results I had gotten earlier, only better. Not only did our own artillery, the V Corps, target us, but the German artillery joined them. Fortunately we were not hit.

The lieutenant gave the cease fire order and like I had done previously, started over from scratch again. Our artillery fired for effect and the lieutenant gave the adjustment. In a few seconds shrapnel was flying all around our tank. The lieutenant coolly said, "Cease fire." Looking at me, he calmly said, "I'm hit, Norber, in the shoulder."

Quickly dropping down into the turret I reached into the gunner's sponson and grabbed the first aid kit. I asked the lieutenant to please remove his jacket so I could apply a bandage to stop any bleeding. But paying no attention to his needs he turned to me and said, "Well, it looks like it's up to you two now, but I'll sure see to it that you get some help up here."

Suddenly feeling woozy and sick to his stomach from the pain in his shoulder, he decided it was time for the medics.

After he was gone, Mac and I sat around and talked a while and kept watch. And while we were watching, an M10 tank destroyer pulled up to join us on the hill and a squad of infantrymen filed into the trench up ahead of us. It was late now and darkness had enshrouded the area making activity on the hill unobservable to the enemy. In talking about our situation, we both knew our problems were being solved for us and we felt that we would sometime soon be receiving another tank commander and driver to fill out our crew.

One of the major problems we hadn't gotten to talk about with Lieutenant Cullin was our battery problem. Simply put, our battery was so weak it should have been replaced, and it would have been, had not the urgency of the Bergstein battle necessitated our being on the line instead of being back at ordinance for refitting. In addition to our battery, which went completely dead at times, our Homelite (battery charger) could not be turned on by depressing its electric starter button. At these "dead" times our Homelite was turned on by manually cranking it with a rope. Since the it was installed in the loader's sponson, it was Mac's job to turn it on. Unfortunately, the rope needed to crank it could not be safely and securely stored in the sponson near him, so it was kept tied to the luggage rack outside the turret within easy reach of the tank commander. This make-shift arrangement was the best possible arrangement that could be made.

Sitting in the darkness, obscured from the enemy, Mac and I thought of our electricity problems, but we never considered turning the Homelite on to recharge our battery because the sound of its "putt-putt" motor could be heard by the Germans who could pinpoint fire on us. The thought of us being a stationary target in a driverless tank wasn't too comforting, but the thought of us sitting there without any communication was even less comforting.

Figuring the drain on our battery caused by keeping our radio receiver on briefly would be negligible and wanting to be in communication so I could receive radio warning, I decided to keep the receiver on. As the night wore on, however, I found myself becoming more anxious about the battery than our communications, so I turned the receiver off.

Aside from my anxiety, it made sense to keep it off because radio silence was usually maintained as much as possible during the night. Besides, if I heard radio noises coming from the nearby tank destroyer's receiver, I could snap on our own receiver momentarily to pick up the message. Shortly after our radio was turned off, a runner came up to our tank to inform me that our company commander wanted to see me back at the Infantry Command Post.

Arriving at the command post I saw Lieutenant Rollins standing among some half-blasted down walls. Lieutenant Rollins stood next to Lieutenant Cullin. I was surprised to see Lieutenant Cullin because I thought he would have been evacuated by now, so after reporting in to Lieutenant Rollins, I turned to Lieutenant Cullin and asked him how he was feeling and what he was doing up here.

Lieutenant Cullin said that he was just up with Lieutenant Rollins making a last check of our platoon and arranging to get me help so we could meet the German counterattack, which was probably going to take place in the morning.

Lieutenant Rollins took over briefing me on the disposition of our armor. On my left and slightly to my rear were situated most of our company's tanks. Sergeant Verhagen, in one of those tanks, was again our platoon leader. My armored vehicle was still the point tank and to my left, right and direct fronts were the enemy. "You can fire freely at anything that moves out there. One last word: on the right, friendly infantry is going to try to move up during the night." In the darkness they were hoping to draw abreast of me straightening our front line.

From his orientation briefing, Lieutenant Rollins turned to the urgent needs of my tank.

"Sometime soon you are going to get a driver and gunner, but before that, we're sending you someone to fix your fuel line." When it appeared very likely that our tank would again be movable, I asked for permission to run my Homelite to recharge the battery.

Lieutenant Rollins denied this request saying, "You are to maintain radio silence during the night. In that way your battery may be strong enough to turn your motor on in the morning when the Germans counterattack. In any event, once the battle starts, you can turn on the Homelite or radio, and anything else you can get on. But for now, just keep silent."

I really had no big worries about being out of communication during the night because practically nothing came over the radio at that time that would affect me. I felt certain the Germans would never attack during the night, but would wait until morning and by then, I would be back in communication.

One last requirement that was being taken care of was my ammunition needs. "You'll come over here to get your ammo," Lieutenant Rollins was saying. "It's too dangerous for the ammo truck or track to go to your tank, too much open ground." I could well understand that if the ammo carrier was hit, our whole position would become jeopardized.

The defense of Bergstein had been looked at from different angles. Even Lieutenant Rollins' order to maintain silence at the crest of the hill had been well thought out: "You're not in full view of the Germans and from what they see, they might think your tank isn't manned, so don't tip them off by running the Homelite."

Carrying a case of three 75mm shells on my back across 75 yards of open field proved to be a real adrenalin raiser. While walking near the T.D. (tank destroyer) on the crest line, the Germans decided it was a perfect time to attack. As the shells exploded around me, the earth rumbled and I fell to the ground several times dropping my ammo. In addition to this indirect shelling, the Germans were also aiming directly at the tank destroyer, which was returning fire and maneuvering around trying to get in track defilade. During their maneuvering the T.D. received two ricocheting hits on its suspension system which sent sparks showering out at the bottom of its suspension system. At any rate, the T.D. was the big target at which the Germans were aiming in the moonlight, and despite being hit twice, the T.D. boldly jockeyed around the crest of the hill, backing off only a few feet trying to get in track defilade.

It was awesome with so much direct and indirect fire falling in our area. With indirect fire I could at least hit the ground as I heard the whine of the high trajectory incoming shell, but with direct fire, all I heard was the shell cutting through the air around me as it passed and a second or so later, I heard the report of the gun that fired it. At any rate, as soon as our tank got resupplied with ammo, the flare-up on the crest unaccountably ceased and all was quiet.

During this quiet period, the help Lieutenant Rollins promised arrived at our tank and preparations for the German counterattack got underway.

The first to arrive was Aarvo Rautanen, a tank driver from another platoon, who had volunteered to repair the ruptured fuel line. While he was busy clamping the line, my new crew arrived.

Ed Walter, who had been Bill Aldy's assistant driver during Tennessee Maneuvers, was now my driver; James Stump, who promptly informed me that he had been a driver and a loader before but never a gunner, was now my new gunner; and the last man who reported in to become my assistant driver, was a replacement whom I'd never seen before. Unfortunately, I don't remember this man's name. Knowing that the assistant driver's hatch was sealed shut, I explained to my would-be assistant driver that his services would not be required because he couldn't get out of the tank in time to keep from being blown up in case we were further disabled.

Somehow my explanation didn't seem to satisfy this young replacement, and he countered me with, "I want to help, and Lieutenant Rollins said." It was obvious he had volunteered to help like the others, so I gratefully thanked him and told him how much we all appreciated his willingness to stay, but with the hatch sealed (which I doubted Lieutenant Rollins knew), I couldn't allow it. Reluctantly he left.

Like most tankers in our company Stump, my replacement gunner knew more about the gun that he had indicated to me when he reported in. Knowing about the manual operation of the weapon, he quickly understood everything about the electrically powered operation and where the different switches and buttons were located. After a few minutes of a crash course with my gunner, it was clear to me I had a gunner who would man the gun properly. All he needed was experience.

We took turns keeping watch and sleeping or trying to sleep that night. Whatever napping was done was accomplished in a sitting up position in our respective tank seats. Resumption of German artillery fire prevented our sleeping alongside or under the tank. It was a scary night and I doubt if anyone in our crew got in very much shut-eye.

In the darkness, my attention was drawn several times to the tank destroyer which was some twenty-five or thirty feet from me. Looking into their open turret, I saw a flickering orange glow appear and heard the static of their radio. They were in communication, receiving messages. I felt they must be of vital importance because extreme caution was being exercised so as to maintain radio silence as much as possible. Several times I wanted to switch my receiver on to pick up the message and had even thought of going over to talk with the T.D. crew, but I knew or hoped if any message affected me it would be conveyed, if they knew I was out of communication. Our setup for communications at the crest of the hill left a lot to be desired.

I was keeping watch, scanning the quiet battlefield that lay stretched before me when I suddenly noticed, in the moonlight, an object moving around some 400 yards away. It was an enemy tank, coming under cover of darkness, heading for our position.

"Gunner, tank, A.P." I started into the fire order. I had the tank right in the center of my turret sight. "Traverse right, steady, traverse left, steady, on." We could hit this baby right now. But so could our tank destroyer, and his high velocity 90mm gun could knock out a tank more easily than could our 75mm which was pretty much ineffective against the front armor of German tanks.

As the T.D. traversed his turret picking up the target simultaneously with me, I saw the flickering orange light going on in his turret, and once more I heard static. He was receiving a message.

While the enemy tank was slowly, very slowly advancing on our position, I couldn't understand why the T.D. didn't open fire immediately. What message was he receiving? The German tank was now two hundred and fifty yards away. Stump was waiting for me to say "Fire!" The T.D. on my left was withholding fire and he was in communication. Continuing to track the tank I commanded "Traverse left, steady on." When the bastard was broadside, if he ever got that close, I'd open up. The orange light in the T.D. was flickering and I could hear the static, what was the message?

"Loader, radio on," I commanded.

Mac switched on the radio. Faintly, yet clearly I heard the words, "..so don't fire, the F.O. (forward observer) is coming up." Was this why the T.D. wasn't firing?

"Three One to Black One," I began calling out to our company commander. Getting no response, I asked Mac if I was getting out.

He assured me I was.

I couldn't believe it was our F.O. coming from that direction. Yet the T.D. was withholding fire, I was stumped! If I opened fire and killed our own F.O. after being told to withhold fire, it would be horrible. I couldn't wait any longer!

"Traverse left, steady on." I had the tank coming at me squarely in my turret sight. The tank was getting perilously close in now, if only I knew for certain it wasn't our own F.O. Stump was quietly waiting all the while for me to say "Fire". There was no way we could miss.

Was it the F.O.? Had our infantry advanced so far during the night and gotten to the right edge of the forest, outflanking the Germans? What the hell? Our radio receiver had been on just long enough for me to clearly make out that message about the F.O. If I hadn't heard that, all the men in the approaching tank would be dead by now.

The questionable tank now was slowly closing, one hundred yards, and now was making a sharp right turn (its right) and was heading for our position on the hill. Now it was almost broadside to us. I could barely make out the helmeted figure in the turret, but the distinct metallic sounds of the tank's treads as it drew closer made me feel certain it was a German tank which was now directly in front of us at thirty or so yards.

The helmeted figure was looking around. What the hell? This is not our F.O.! Why doesn't the T.D. fire??!!

I learned after the war the T.D. delayed firing because of a bulged round in the chamber that had to be removed.

Suddenly the T.D.'s gun roared. He fired, and missed!

"Fire, Stump!" I shouted. Stump fired and hit the German tank squarely, broadside. The explosion was deafening. The Germans clambered out of their tank and scrambled back in the direction from which their tank had come. Up ahead of us from their trench our infantry was opening up on the Germans as they fled from the crest. While this was going on I yelled to Mac, "Was that an H.E.?" (high explosive)

"Yeah," he answered. In the confusion an H.E. instead of an A.P. (armor piercing) had been thrown into the breech. Now as Mac was slamming an A.P. round into the breech, the T.D. opened fired with its powerhouse piece and sent a shell into the German tank, blowing it up. The German tank on blowing up burst into flames and in the glare of the flames, the outlines of the T.D. and my tank could be seen silhouetted against the darkness of the night. Our position was now clearly defined to the enemy.

If the effect of the exploding shells hitting the German tank had been strong on the T.D. and tankers, it must have been doubly strong on the infantrymen who were crouched in the trench just ahead of us, maybe twenty feet from the German tank which was now burning fiercely in the darkness.

In the early daylight hours all hell broke loose. The Germans laid down a tremendous barrage on our position. The T.D., my tank and the squad of infantrymen in the trench ahead of us were blanketed in exploding shells. The T.D. and my tank commenced firing at the German guns.

A voice called out to me from the side of my tank, "Norby, Norby, let me in! Let me in!"

I reached down to lend a helping hand to Billy R., an infantryman who fled his artillery besieged trench. Billy survived the hellish night and had the awful experience of watching the German tank explode and burn. Billy, a good soldier, an infantryman we'd relied on for the past four months, had cracked. Doing the only thing possible with Billy, I had him lie down on the floor of the turret.

After getting him situated I resumed my firing order to Stump. Somehow, as Stump was elevating the barrel of the gun, the breech being depressed, I glanced into the turret and saw Billy sitting with his head between the gun breech and the gun guard.

"Get his head down, get his head down!" I shouted.

If the order to fire had been given, the recoil of the 75mm would have crushed Billy's skull. The gunner's "On the way" warning would have meant nothing to the dazed infantryman.

Now the entire area on my left was being saturated by exploding shells. Around me, direct fire as well as indirect fire was ripping through the air.

Intent on knocking out the German guns firing at us, I gave no order to maneuver the tank, but instead continued dueling with the German artillery pieces.

Sounds of explosions were going on all around me as the enemy artillery continued to rain down on us. In back of me, on our rear deck, a man had scrambled aboard. "Norber, let me in, my tank's been knocked out!" It was Rogers, one of Joe's crew.

At first Rogers seemed not to understand my refusal to let him in. "I've got a man under the gun now."

"It's hell out here!" Rogers exclaimed.

Realizing he didn't know what I said about the man under the gun, I repeated myself and pointed to Billy on the floor under the gun.

Seeing we had no room in the tank, Rogers jumped to the ground and was gone.

The shelling continued unabated. Mac and Stump were urging me to lower myself into the turret, but I remained erect; tall in the turret, so as to have a wider view of the battlefield and be able to pinpoint German artillery. Ordinarily not a fearless man, I knew no fear at this time. Battle can do strange things to people.

The T.D. to my left front was jockeying around. German artillery was zeroing in on us. The fire was withering when I commanded, "Driver, back up!"

"Can't turn 'er over, no juice!" Walter responded.

"Mac, turn the Homelite on!" I ordered.

Mac, who was busy loading the gun now, had another job to do.

My attention at this time was drawn to machine gun fire we were receiving from my right front. Not able to traverse the turret to the right while Mac was working with the Homelite in the left sponson, I swung over 50 caliber on the turret ring in the direction in the tracers had come from and fired.

The pressure from the artillery was unrelenting. "Back up!" I shouted to Walter again.

"Can't back up, no battery!" Walter responded.

At this time Mac leaned near the gun and said, "Can't get Homelite on! Give me the rope."

I took the rope, which was right at hand where Joe kept it on the luggage rack on the back of the turret, and handed it to Mac.

While Mac was trying to get the battery charger started, Stump was left momentarily without a loader, thus reducing our tank's firepower to the lone 50 caliber machine gun on the turret ring which I continued firing.

The air was alive with shrapnel. Suddenly the T.D. a few yards from us was hit and blew up. Fire belched from the open turret and the crewmen, ablaze and screaming, fell over the sides of the burning hulk.

Their screams rent the air as they went staggering by the tracks of my tank, burning torches.

While this was going on I was caught in the turret, caught in an intersecting field of machine gun fire. Short bursts were coming from our left and right fronts.

Again I started ordering Walter to back up and again Walter responded that he had no battery.

We were a sitting duck. We were dead in the water and we'd soon be dead in the war.

"Mac, get that Homelite started!"

Mac came up from the sponson and said, "Can't get the Homelite on. Won't start even with a rope."

In the midst of this unbelievable hell with the sights and sounds of battle all around me, and the screams of men burning alive filling the air, all courage I had ever known in battle left me. Suddenly, my right forearm was gripped by muscle spasms as I was firing the 50 caliber. I started having trouble handling the gun, struggling to keep it elevated so I wouldn't spray our infantry, those left in the trench. I tried desperately to continue firing.

My fingers were now curling away from the butterfly trigger and gun grip and the spasms in my right forearm were extremely severe. My left side was operative, but the fingers of my right hand were becoming so paralyzed that I couldn't work them.

In desperation I shouted again, "Back up!"

"No battery."

Trapped in an immovable tank with artillery fire zeroing in on us, our position was hopeless. Panic-stricken, I leaned into the turret and bellowed, "Abandon tank!"

I got out, stepped on the deck and dropped to the ground on the right side of the tank. In quick order Stump, followed by Billy, joined me. Mac meanwhile was removing the back plates from the 75mm cannon and the 30 co-ax machine gun making them useless should the Germans capture the tank intact. After what seemed an eternity, Mac appeared coming out of the turret on the left side. But Walter, where was he?

I darted to the front of the tank. "Walter!"

The driver's hatch opened and Walter scrambled out and dropped to the ground on the left side of the tank, the driver's side.

For a split second our eyes met as we paused at opposite sides of the tank. At that instant, we heard a loud "Bap!" A direct fire shell had come between Walter and me and penetrated the turret of our tank. Had the order to abandon been delayed thirty seconds, we would all have been added to the already high casualty list at Bergstein.

My nerves completely shattered, I was overcome by the instinct of self-preservation and quickly found myself following Billy into an open field as he led the way toward the Infantry Command Post.

I was now crawling and running through machine gun fire which was attempting to pin Billy and me down. Men all around us were crawling, some moaning from wounds.

It didn't take Billy and me long to reach the Infantry Command Post. The muscle spasms that had gripped my right forearm were now gone and a semblance of sensibility had returned to me. I looked around for Billy. He had disappeared.

Standing on the ground, amid the half-blown down walls, I stood at the top of the stairs and watched as two medics were assisting a man with a gaping hole in his chest down the stairs. The man was Van Arkel, and though he was in great agony, he was mumbling to the medics, "Leave me, save yourselves!"

After the medics got Van in the basement, I went down the steps and heard the moaning of the horribly burned T.D. men. They were stretched out on the floor and medical aid men were attending them. Turning from this scene, I went into another room, where the platoon leader of the infantry was talking to me. "My men are having trouble identifying German tanks from ours. Can you help?"

I took his field glasses from him and went up the stairs, knelt on a narrow ledge behind part of a blown down wall. Out in no-man's land, a tank was milling around. Quickly I put the field glasses to my eyes.

"German tank, 200 yards!"

I had spotted the tank with its markings first, but even as I spotted them, they spotted me. The tank fired at me. The shell slammed into the bricks. The bricks flew, mortar from between the bricks flew into my open mouth, the field glasses were dropped.

An infantryman who'd been standing in the basement beneath me helped break my fall as I fell from the ledge above him. After steadying myself I found my mouth was dry and grimy. Bits of mortar that had seconds before supported the bricks of the rubble I'd stood behind, were now sprayed in my throat and throughout my hair. I was half in shock and I could hardly speak.

I walked back to the room which the infantry lieutenant was using as his headquarters. On hearing my report that I'd seen a German tank but no American tanks, the lieutenant walked to the doorway of the room and in a calm and collected manner called out, "Prepare to withdraw! Get the wounded ready. We'll load the half-tracks."

After helping to lift some of the wounded, I stood along a half blown down wall in the rubble of what had been the Infantry Command Post and watched as the first two half-tracks loaded down with their wounded sped off bound for a medical aid station in the rear.

After those two tracks were gone one half-track remained to carry us, the able-bodied, to God knows where. By this time I was so dazed and confused that I had to be urged by the men already in the carrier to mount up. Being the last man to board, I felt the track starting to roll as I put my foot on the top of the track as I balanced myself before entering the bed of the carrier.

As we sped down the road, I was dimly aware of shots being fired, then hearing someone say that Young, the Platoon Sergeant commanding our half-track, had shot some Germans who had risen up from both sides of the road to ambush us. *(While visiting Platoon Sergeant Young in 1981, he told me that he was driving the half track and someone else fired at the Germans).*

Now the track was stopped. I didn't know if it was hit, was over on its side, or what. Men all around me were abandoning the vehicle and were running down the road, so I just took off following them. Seconds later, the road was being peppered by German artillery and all of us were sprawling, rising, and running, trying to get to any building for cover.

I made it to the ground floor of a demolished building, where I was pausing to catch my breath, when up popped Billy. Where he came from I didn't know. In front of us were several infantrymen just sitting on the ground talking as unconcernedly as though they were back in some barracks in the States. Billy was telling them, "One over, one short, we're bracketed!" Billy spoke directly to the unconcerned soldiers.

In reply they sneered at him, saying "You battle-fatigued or something?" and resumed talking among themselves, completely ignoring Billy.

It's possible we were a good mile or so from the Bergstein ridge, but just because only two shells had been fired at our position didn't mean we weren't in a dangerous spot. We were bracketed!

"The next one's coming right in here, follow me." And Billy led me to a huge hole in the floor, to an exposed beam. Hanging by the beam, he dropped into the basement. I followed.

From the back of the basement came the sound of voices. Medics were working on some wounded. Upstairs all was quiet but not for long. In less than a minute a deafening blast hit the area over us, and the basement shook. A soldier's bloody legs appeared hanging from the beam followed by the rest of him as he fell into the basement. Some medics were coming over to him.

Billy said, "We'll go up and check when the air's clear."

Back upstairs, my friend and I stood looking at the remains of four or five dead soldiers, their helmets blown off, their heads lopsided and bodies mangled. And Billy was saying remorsefully, "They should'a listened, they should'a listened."

The next thing I remember is standing among some debris alongside a road and several men were congregating around me. I had lost track of Billy or he had lost track of me. One of the men, a medic, I believe, was saying, "You gott'a go to the rear. You gott'a be evacuated."

In shock and unable to function, my condition was obvious to him. Though I was completely exhausted, confused and disoriented, one small group of cells tucked away in some inner sanctum of my brain controlled me. My conscience simply wouldn't permit me to be evacuated while horribly burned men were waiting for transportation to the rear. I couldn't take up a place that could be used by them.

In shock, I wandered into a room somewhere. Friendly G.I.'s, maybe three, four, five or six of them were in this room. The room became a basement. I was in a basement, and I was sleeping. Slowly I became aware of my surroundings. Occasionally, shells burst in the street above us. Once I overheard a couple of infantrymen talking, "Whaddeya mean you just let those two Krauts walk away! After they walk in here and surrender, you just let them go? What the hell?!"

And the other one was saying, "They'll be back, you'll see. It's worse over on their side. You'll see 'em come runnin' back to us pretty soon." Then there was laughter.

Even though I was too comatose or whatever to catch the humor, I nevertheless sensed that the basement we were holed up in was a safe place. At times one of the G.I.'s would awaken me from my zombie-like state and try to get me to eat something. At other times he would ask if I ever had to go. I don't remember ever having a bite to eat or perform any bodily function while there.

After spending possibly two or three nights in the basement, I was awakened suddenly. "Get up, get up, the Rangers are here." The U.S. 2nd Ranger Battalion, crack troops who had scaled the cliffs on the beaches of Normandy during the invasion had arrived to relieve us.

The nightmare of Bergstein was over. It was behind us. The remnants of our outfit were now bivouacked in some sort of a rest area, sleeping in pup tents. For me, I was completely exhausted and there could be no restful sleep. I would never be the same man I was prior to Bergstein. The sights and sounds, the horrors of the battlefield, the burning, screaming human torches were ever present in my mind. For all practical purposes my soldiering days ended at Bergstein.

THROUGH BATTLE FATIGUED EYES

It was night, I believe, and I was somewhere behind the lines in a school building that was being used as a hospital. The schoolroom I was in had been made into a ward and on one of the beds in this ward I was sleeping. Suddenly, the darkness was interrupted. Light flooded the room and I heard my name being called.

I rose from my bed and in a half-sleep made my way to the doctor's desk.

"Sit down on the chair, corporal." The voice was firm, yet courteous.

"Why did you wake me in the middle of the night?"

"What do you want to do, corporal?"

I was crying, bawling. "I want to go back to my company. I've got to get back to my company."

The doctor said nothing in reply.

Moments later I was back in bed, drifting into sleep.

The following morning some 200 to 400 men stood in formation in a large schoolyard. An officer, standing in the center of the yard, called out two or three names. Mine was one. Soon I was in an ambulance. I was on my way back to my outfit.

Much later in the evening of the same day I was entering a two-story house when I was stopped.

"Hey, where do you think you're going?" The platoon sergeant look worn and tired, but his greeting was friendly. He was one of the infantrymen who had emerged from the forest with me.

"I'm reporting back for duty, but I don't know who's around to report to," I told him.

"Captain Pool is upstairs."

"Captain Pool... you mean he's back? Why, he was a bloody mess when the medics evacuated him!"

"Yeah, I know, I know, but he's back and he's o.k. Listen, I tried to tell him you weren't coming back, but he wouldn't hear of it. All I know is he said he wanted to see you as soon as you get back, that's what he told me."

The sergeant and I walked up the stairs. At the top of the stairs was a hallway, and off the hallway were two or three rooms. He opened the door to one of the rooms.

"I'll leave you now," he said. "Captain Pool's expecting you."

The room was well lit and the shades were drawn. Across the room sitting on the floor, his back again the wall, was Captain Pool. Seated alongside him also propped against the wall were several other officers. It was obvious from their appearance that their conversation was informal.

The captain looked well enough for a man who'd recently been hit by mortar and machine gun fire and lost a good deal of blood; but the captain always looked well. Sitting on the floor, his long, lean Texan frame was not too much in evidence, and the upper half of his body appeared unusual – somewhat bulky – but that was because he was heavily bandaged about his chest and one arm.

I'd walked to within a couple of feet of where the captain was seated before he turned his head from the group and suddenly saw me.

"Norber!" he exclaimed. "We were just talking about you a few minutes ago." The tone of his voice indicated that he was happy to see me again. "How are you?"

"Fine, thanks," I replied. Though I was confused and deeply troubled, my reply was nonetheless perfunctory.

"Won't you have a seat and join us?" The captain said. "We're just discussing a book, The Robe. You read it?"

"No, I haven't," I replied. "What's it about?"

"The robe of Christ.."

"The robe of Christ? What's that?" I asked.

"You know, the robe, the robe the centurions shot dice on at the crucifixion. You know, the story from the Bible."

"Oh, from the Bible." I could feel myself becoming uneasy. I'd never read the Bible, so I wasn't versed enough to know of the robe.

Somehow, though, without his realizing it, with this opening shot the captain had struck home. A great deal of what was troubling me at the time was not The Bible, but belief. I wanted to talk to Captain Pool about what to believe in, but I didn't care to talk where others were present.

"Captain Pool, is there some place I could talk privately with you?" I asked.

"Sure," he said, and with that he got to his feet and we left the room and walked into the hallway; at the end of the hallway where there was a window. The moonlight shining through the window was our only source of light. We were to ourselves, where we could talk without being overheard.

Standing there facing the captain, I didn't know where to start or what to say. In my mind, I could hear the screaming of burning men; in my mind I could see my best friend being killed by an artillery burst; in my mind I could see myself crawling through machine gun fire in a field littered with the wounded and dying, and in my sickened mind I could make no sense out of any of it. I reached into my shirt pocket and fumbled with my prayer book. I could almost feel the Star of David that was imprinted on it. I moved the prayer book aside and felt what was behind it: a crumpled picture of Christ I'd picked up at the hospital. My thought surfaced.

"Captain," I said, "I don't know what to believe or believe in." I hesitated, and I asked him, "Do you ever pray?"

And he replied, "Yes."

"Well, what do you pray for?" I asked.

"Two things: courage and a clear mind," he replied.

I said, "I still don't know what to believe or believe in."

His response was immediate. "You do your best on earth and the rest is taken care of for you."

"Would you mind telling me what your religion is?" I asked.

"I'm a Unitarian," he said.

"A Unitarian? I've never heard of that before." I don't recall his reply, or maybe I didn't hear any because I was thinking: "It's probably a Texas sect of some sort and I probably shouldn't be asking questions like this of a Texan. Too personal!"

I didn't concern myself further with the name of the captain's religion or sect or whatever it was, but I did reflect on the things he valued: things like courage and a clear mind. And what little comfort I could find in words or thought I found in the thought that one could do one's best and the rest was taken care of for him.

With religious problems settled, the two of us turned to military problems. The captain spoke of a massive counter-offensive the Germans had launched in the Ardennes. The Germans, he said, were enjoying some immediate successes, but whatever successes they may be enjoying, Bergstein was not one of them.

It was what Captain Pool said next that disturbed me. "Now that we're talking here, I have something to tell you: you're going to be a tank commander."

That especially I didn't want to hear. "Captain Pool," I protested, "I'm a gunner and I'd like to continue to be a gunner."

The captain started to say something about there being a need for good tank commanders but suddenly he caught himself. Perhaps he sensed my lack of self-confidence: something he'd never sensed before, perhaps he sensed my extreme weariness. I don't know what it was that caused him to immediately drop the matter, but very quickly he changed tack.

"Corporal Norber," his words came evenly, "I think you need a good break, and I'm going to see to it that you get one. Sometime tomorrow you're going back to a rear rest area and you're going to do nothing but relax for a few days. Then after you're all rested up, you'll come back to the company and at that time we'll talk about this matter further. Now, if you decide at that time that you'd rather be a gunner than a tank commander, then I'll go along with your decision." The captain hesitated momentarily, and glanced at his watch. "Right now it's late, and I suggest you get some sleep, and, oh, yes, did I tell you – I'm glad you came back!"

We shook hands and he walked into the shadowy darkness of the hallway, returning to the room from which we'd emerged a few minutes earlier.

I was standing alone in the hallway staring out the window into a starry night and for a moment, my eyes fell on a small group of snow-blanketed fir trees. It was Christmas time. Peace on earth, good will to men.

I didn't hear my friend come up behind me, but suddenly I was aware of his presence. I turned and looked into his deep brown eyes. It was the last time I'd ever see him alive, and all he asked of me was a simple request. "Will you write my mother for me, Vic?"

"I can't right now, Bill, but I will later." But later never came and I broke a promise.

On the following morning I moved to a rest area; a handful of pyramid tents pitched in a quiet wooded area, surrounded by very tall trees. Detached from the company and released from duty, I passed the daylight hours walking and wandering among the trees, trying to relax and forget the horrors of the recent past. But the horrors that gripped my mind were not easily forgotten, for my mind was in too much of a sickened state to dispel them. After spending a few days in the rest area I returned to my company. On reporting in to Captain Pool, I asked that I be allowed to return to the company as a tank gunner. My request was granted.

One night not long after my return to duty, my tank moved up to an outpost. It was a relatively quiet sector of the combat zone we moved into. Sometime in the night a few shells fell nearby. And sometime during the shelling I thought one of my friends was blown apart. When the shelling ceased, I left the tank to walk to the Infantry Command Post which was nearby. There had been no casualties. The only person affected by the minor shelling had been me. I wasn't myself anymore.

In the Infantry Command Post someone was saying that Captain Pool had been radioed and was on his way.

Shortly afterwards, Captain Pool was talking to me in a room adjoining that of the Infantry Command Post. We were to ourselves again.

I was sitting down on a chair or a bench and I was half in tears.

"Have you shot your wad, Norber?" The captain's voice was calm, friendly.

"Yes."

"Are you afraid to sleep out here tonight?"

"No."

"I'll see you tomorrow morning."

REMEMBRANCE OF A FAREWELL

"The captain is here, Norber. He's outside waiting for you in his peep. "I went outside to greet him. It was a bright morning and snow was on the ground.

"Just throw your bedroll in back."

I tossed my bedroll in. Odd, about the bedroll. Odd, how such a simple thing as rolling a bedroll was too difficult for me to do. The new men in the platoon, or was it the infantrymen, had rolled it for me.

"Are you ready to go, Corporal Norber?" The captain was friendly.

I had already checked my pockets a couple of times and made sure the extractor from the 30 caliber machine gun wasn't on me. I felt sure this time I'd put it where it belonged—in the bolt.

It was a short ride back to the battalion dispensary. When we stopped the captain told me he would have to say goodbye now—that I was to go into the dispensary and wait for other transportation that would take me elsewhere. So I stepped out of the peep and walked toward the dispensary. I must have gone fifteen or twenty feet when I heard him call, "Corporal Norber."

"Yes?"

"Aren't you going to shake hands with me?"

"Oh? Yes."

"Goodbye, Corporal Norber," he said. And he gripped my hand firmly.

"I'll see you in two months," I said.

"Yes. I'll see you in two months," he replied, "in St. Louis."

I was disoriented, disorganized, and completely exhausted, but I knew my condition: I was in contact with reality, and certain that with proper rest I would return within two months.

An ambulance took me from the dispensary and drove me to another building somewhere. My thoughts were clear as the morning air when I entered the building.

I was in a room when the major came in and introduced himself, saying he was the Division psychiatrist and that he would like to talk with me for a few minutes.

I sat on a chair next to his desk.

His first question was simple. "Where did you come from?"

"The dispensary," I replied.

He asked me some tough questions: which direction did I come from; what was the name of the place in the line I had come from before I reached the dispensary; and what day it was. Questions that seemed unimportant, irrelevant, and unanswerable. I admitted I hadn't been too sharp lately, and he switched to other subjects. Mostly we discussed things about "after battle effects," how I felt physically, my background, and once or so we went all the way back to my childhood. Even as he wrote his notes, I believe the major knew that for the most part my thinking processes were still intact.

At the conclusion of the interview he led me into another room, showed me where my bed would be for the time being, and told me to make myself comfortable. That night for the first time since the holocaust, I slept soundly in my assigned bed.

On the following morning after breakfast, I was preparing to take leave. I was standing in the hallway near the door, waiting for an ambulance that was to take me elsewhere and listening to the major's instructions.

"You are to wear this envelope around your neck next to your dog tags," he was saying, and as he spoke he looped a string over my head that was attached to a large messenger envelope. "This way," he continued, "you won't lose it. On your way back to your destination there will be doctors who will want to read the contents of this envelope, so you'll let them have the envelope when they request it. Any questions?"

I wasn't interested in the envelope at the time, but I did have a question in mind that bothered me quite a bit.

"They won't lock me up, will they major?"

The major smiled reassuringly. "No, corporal, I'm sure you won't be locked up."

The door to the hallway opened and an ambulance driver entered and walked up to the major. "Is the patient ready?"

The major said, "Yes," and then looked at me and said, "Goodbye, corporal, and good luck."

And I was on my way.

THE ENVELOPE

Somewhere in France a train rolled noiselessly through the night. Inside a sleeper coach I awoke to dim lights. I was lying on a low metal bunk only a few inches above the floor. I looked about me. The coach, though dimly lit, had blackout curtains drawn over the windows, blotting out the night. The swaying of the Paris-bound train, as it hummed over the rails, had gently rocked me to consciousness.

The envelope hung loosely about my neck. It attracted my attention. I wondered what was in it that was so important. The envelope was unsealed. The flap at the top of the envelope was held down by a small string that was strapped around a small cardboard disc that was stapled to the lower part of the envelope. I unloosen the string, lifted the flap, and drew out the sheet of paper that was enclosed.

TO A.P.O. 255

This man was with us when we entered Normandy. He has always been an excellent and reliable gunner. He has never shown any act of cowardice.

Signed: Capt. F. M. Pool, Commanding Officer

B Co. 10th Tank Battalion

And underneath this ran the major's notes, which read something like this:

COMBAT: Soldier has undergone four and one half months severe combat.

History of Patient: Mother died from heart ailment when patient was eleven years old. Father is living. Patient has one older brother and one older sister. Following mother's death family experienced severe financial problems which led to family breakup. Patient and sister sent to foster home. As a child, patient bit fingernails.

Physical symptoms: Patient has floating sensations, surroundings seem to float. At night he sometimes is awakened by cramping of muscles (spasms) over entire body. Such attacks began shortly after unit first saw action; however, attacks have recently escalated occurring four or five times a night. Patient says he has seen a deceased tank commander's head atop other soldiers' bodies.

Note: This was an erroneous interpretation of what I said. The major had asked if I ever thought I'd seen Joe, my former tank commander, after he was killed. In reply, I said that once I saw someone who looked like him; his back was to me and he was standing in line. When I walked over to where this soldier was standing, he turned around, and when I saw his face, I knew it wasn't him. That was the only error I saw among the major's notes.

After skimming the major's notes I returned to the captain's statement at the top of the sheet. I thought about the captain's opening line: that I had been with the outfit since it landed in Normandy. The statement was true, of course, but actually I'd been with the outfit since March of 1942, which was twenty-eight months previous to our landing in Normandy. I wondered why the captain hadn't mentioned that, but it really didn't matter to me.

My curiosity regarding the contents of the envelope settled. I returned the paper to the envelope and lay back on my bunk.

While lying there resting and reflecting, I returned to my record several times, reading and re-reading Captain Pool's brief remarks addressed to the A.P.O. 255. I did not read my record surreptitiously, but did so openly, for I had no thought or care of anyone's watching me. The fact that my reading of my record was or could be construed as a wrongdoing never occurred to me.

A huge monstrous stone structure hung suspended in mid-air in a gray-black Parisian night. It faced an undulating sea of exhausted humanity that rolled and floundered before its closed doors. At a given moment, the doors to the edifice swung open and a sea of khaki-clad men swirled into the hospital.

Admittedly, I don't recall entering the hospital in Paris. Because I was completely worn out and beat with intermittent spells of dizziness, I do not recall my being processed for admittance into the hospital, but I do recall the events that occurred immediately after being admitted.

Once inside the hospital and past the processing stage, I found myself along with several others being escorted up a winding stairway to an open ward on an upper floor. When we entered the ward we found it darkened. Because it was late at night, the overhead lights were out, and most of the patients in the ward appeared to be sleeping. Noiselessly, we, the new patients, were ushered down a long, narrow aisle that ran between the hospital beds. The footlights on the beds gave light to our pathway.

I had barely become situated, just sitting on the side of my bed, when a nurse appeared at my side, handing me a pair of white pajamas saying, "You are allowed to have one or two sleeping pills. Which do you prefer, one or two?"

"One," I replied, thinking I should go easy on the pills.

"You can have two, if you wish," she replied.

I reconsidered, and said, "Okay, then, make it two."

"I'll be back with your pills in a couple of minutes," she said, and she turned and headed back down the long aisle toward the entrance of the ward. She'd gotten maybe twenty feet away, when I suddenly decided I wanted what I'd originally asked for. "Oh nurse," I called.

She stopped and retraced her steps to me. "Yes?"

"I've decided I'd rather have one pill."

The nurse accepted my big decision and went on her way.

While she was gone, I lay back to rest and reflect: "*Clean white sheets in an immaculate hospital ward. I'll rest well in Paris, and if I'm lucky, I may even be transferred to some unit in Paris; that is, after I'm well-rested.*" *That's as far as my thoughts went.*

"Hey, Mac!"

I looked around. The patient in the bed next to mind was addressing me. His eyes showed fright as he looked imploringly into mine. "Get two pills, Mac, please," he whispered. "I can't sleep. Battle dreams. Please, get two pills and give me one. They won't give me any pills. Please, they'll give you two."

The sound of desperation in his voice – the nightly terrors. How well I knew those terrors.

I looked down the aisle, the nurse was returning with my pill. When she reached my bed I spoke in a low voice, so as not to disturb other sleeping patients. "I hate to bother you, but I've changed my mind again. I really think I'd better have two pills."

"No bother," she replied. "It'll just take a minute more for me to get it."

In a few seconds she was back. This time she handed me two pills and a glass of water. I swallowed one pill and cupped the other. When the nurse was gone I handed the leftover pill to "battle dreams."

Morning came suddenly. The lights switched on and I heard my name being called from the front of the ward. Before I could answer, I heard my name being called again. "Coming," I yelled, and swung my legs out of bed and made my way to the front of the ward and the doctor's desk.

The doctor was pleasant. "Did you sleep well last night, Corporal?"

"Yes sir, very well."

"How many sleeping pills did you have?"

Mentally, I recalled the night before. I knew I'd taken one, but I also knew the nurse had handed me two. "I took one... no," I thought again, "two." I correct myself, then "one or two."

The puzzled doctor looked at me. "You don't remember exactly?"

"No sir, or, yes sir."

"That is all for now, corporal," the doctor replied.

Some time later that morning I got the urge to write a letter to my father to let him know I was in Paris and was in good shape.

On inquiring, I learned that there was a shop downstairs where I could get some stationery. We were located on the second floor at the head of a winding marble stairway. At the foot of this stairway was this shop. Well-oriented, I made my way down the winding marble staircase that led from our ward to the first floor shop. In a few minutes, I was back upstairs with a stationery tablet. Sitting in bed, all set to write, I suddenly realized I had forgotten to get a writing implement. So, I hurried back downstairs for a pencil or pen. After returning to my bed, it dawned on me that I needed envelopes. So it was back downstairs; this time for envelopes. When I'd returned to my bed again I'd had all the things I needed to write a letter.

Only then I decided I ought to find out if that shop had any postcards, because I really didn't feel up to writing a letter.

At the top of the marble stairway, just off the side of the entrance to our ward was the nurses' station. On about my fourth, fifth, or sixth trip up and down the stairway, a nurse emerged from her station and interrupted my travels.

"The doctor has asked me to tell you," she said, "that you are to stay at your bed the rest of the morning. Please don't leave the ward; you are going to be shipped back to England on the first transportation available."

My dreams of being stationed in Paris for the duration of the war had quickly evaporated.

ALMOST HEAVEN

It was night again; the air was crisp and the friendly English stars twinkling. Outside the sprawling expanse of low-level, one-story buildings which formed a U.S. Army base hospital, a large group of battle fatigued solders stood, waiting admittance to the hospital. Inside the hospital, lights were burning and doctors, presumably psychiatrists, were scanning the medical records of the waiting men.

Those of us standing outside the hospital were at ease. We could talk if we wished, smoke if we desired, or just plain think, if we were so inclined. For my part, I came close to thinking. Sometimes gazing at the stars, sometimes gazing aimlessly at the hospital lights, and sometimes staring into the darkness of the hour, I contemplated nothing, but I felt good and I felt calm watching the night.

"I'm Captain Wilks, and I'm the doctor in charge of this ward. Won't you men be seated?" There were two of us to be interviewed and that seemed uncommon. The captain, though, was just an ordinary appearing, friendly doctor, and his office was just an ordinary doctor's office. Yet, it seemed odd that another fatigued soldier and I were going to be interviewed in the office at the same time.

The two of us, the other fatigued soldier and I, sat facing the doctor. First the doctor looked at me. "How long were you in combat?" he asked.

"Somewhat over four months," I replied.

He turned to the man seated next to me and asked him the same question.

As the patient started to reply, I turned in his direction and saw trembling hands, gray-streaked hair, and a deeply lined face. At first the man hesitated in replying, then he mumbled something about having been in a combat zone four or five days, but he added he had never seen any actual combat.

Captain Wilks, sensing the man's discomfort, immediately injected his philosophy on fatigue. Everyone had his limits, the captain said, and whether those limits were reached after four or five minutes in a combat zone, or four or five days in a combat zone, or four or five months in combat, was of no consequence to him as a doctor.

At that I took an instant liking to Wilks.

After expressing his view on fatigue, Captain Wilks returned to me. "What do you like to do for enjoyment or relaxation, Corporal?" he asked.

"I like to read," I replied.

"Are you able to read at this time; I mean, can you concentrate enough to read?"

"I think so."

After answering that question I don't recall any further questioning during the interview; however, I do recall that the three of us sat and chatted amicably for several minutes, after which time the captain informed us that he was assigning us to his ward.

"The ward is open," the captain said, "which means you'll not be restricted to the ward. You'll eat your meals at the hospital's main mess hall, and you'll be able to spend a good deal of time away from the ward. Of course, if, when I make my rounds in the morning, I tell you that I want to see you later in the day, I'll expect you to be on the ward at that time. And for the first few days I may want to see more of you that I will later on. And, oh, yes, we've plenty of good books on the ward, so if you feel like reading, I believe you'll be able to find something to your liking. Any questions?"

Since there were no questions, the captain went to the door, summoned an attendant, and instructed him to show us to our beds in the ward.

After I got my pajamas on, the attendant handed me one or two blue 88's (sleeping pills) and shortly after that I was sleeping soundly. The nightmare of Bergstein and the Hurtgen Forest completely blotted out.

Nothing could have had a more healthful effect on me than the living conditions, or therapies, the doctor made available to me. For several days I lounged around the ward reading books, listening to the radio, and talking with other patients. When I felt the need for fresh air, I would leave the ward and take a relaxing walk in the fresh winter air. Memories of battle had receded and I felt I was beginning to heal in this atmosphere of total relaxation.

And one day my ease was interrupted. I was sitting on my bed contemplating the title of a book I was reading. The book was Under a Lucky Star, and I was thinking how well the title applied to me; for given my circumstances, I felt I myself was under a lucky star. I was in a euphoric mood when somehow I became distracted by the conversations of some patients who were sitting nearby.

"Captain Wilks," one of the patients was saying, "is a battle fatigue case himself. All his patients ever talk about is battle; all his medical buddies talk about is battle. He's so damned surrounded with battle talk, he's become sick himself."

This sad bit of news upset me, because I liked this kindly doctor very much. So I started thinking about it, wondering if there was anything I could do to help him. After giving the matter a little thought, I hit upon the solution. He's got to be mentally removed from this circle of doom. He's got to have outside ideals to lift him from his immediate family of sick men and medical associates. He has to be looking onward and upward: *If I ever get the chance to talk with him, I'll help him.*

No sooner thought than done. An attendant approached my bed and said, "Captain Wilks wants to see you in his office."

Before the interview got underway, I sat looking into the face of the kindly physician I'd come to know and like from the few times we'd exchanged words during morning rounds. He had always been friendly, and he showed a friendly face now, but now I sensed I knew him better. For now I knew that behind that friendly face lurked a sick, sick mind.

"Corporal Norber," Wilks said as he opened the interview, "how do you find our ward?"

"Oh, I find it just fine. I like the relaxed atmosphere of the ward, my freedom to move about, and, oh yes, the books occupy a good portion of my day. What could be better?"

"How are your nights?"

"My nights are just fine, sir."

"Do you have any battle dreams?"

"No, sir. None whatsoever. I guess the sleeping pills are doing their job."

The captain seemed pleased to hear that everything was going so well with me.

"Corporal Norber, I want to ask you a few questions concerning your family and background," he said, looking at my record he held before him. "Let's see, now," he said, reading from my chart. "Your mother died from a heart ailment when you were eleven."

"Yes, sir."

"Did she ever have any other serious ailments?"

"Yes, sir. Infantile paralysis."

"Any others, such as diabetes, arthritis, or any you know of?"

"No, sir."

"Now, after she died you went to live in a foster home. Were these relatives or people you were acquainted with?"

"No, sir. A children's bureau placed my sister and me there."

"And how did you like this foster family, did you like them?"

"No, sir," I replied matter-of-factly, "I did not."

"How many people were there in the family?"

"Five," I answered. And I added, "The foster parents and their two sons and a daughter."

"And you didn't like any of them?" he repeated himself.

At that moment, like a bolt from the blue, it hits me. "_Outward and upward_, I thought, _"Captain Wilks must learn to look outward and upward_." So, in reconsidering the question, I replied thoughtfully that I liked one of the sons. It was a lie, but a white lie; a lie designed to help Captain Wilks with his own personal problems.

"Which son did you like?" the captain was interested. "The older or the younger?"

"The young one, I replied.

"How old was he?"

"About six years older than I."

After jotting down my last reply, the captain sat and appeared to be meditating. While he sat meditating I was feeling very good. Wilks would learn from me, I was sure. He'd see that I'd looked outside my own family; outward and upward. I knew he'd get the message and it would have a good effect on him. Now he'd look away from his small family associated with the battle-fatigued world.

After a few moments the captain resumed. "Now I'd like to ask you a few questions about your time in combat. Do you feel up to answering a few questions for me?"

"Yes, sir."

"I see you were a gunner in a tank. Is that correct?"

"Yes, sir."

"Were you *always* a gunner?" He stressed the words "always,"

On this I hesitated. "Well, once I commanded a tank, but it was only for a short time. Captain Pool didn't know about that." This, of course, was untrue.

"I see," said Captain Wilks, and he saw much more than he cared to divulge at the time. It was obvious to him that I'd read my record. Had he asked me if I'd read my chart I would have said "yes."

However, Captain Wilks did not pursue the issue; instead, he referred to my record and asked me something he already knew.

"And you were in combat for over four months?"

"Yes sir, either in combat or a combat zone."

The index finger on either my right or left hand started jerking involuntarily. On seeing this, Captain Wilks suddenly changed course. "I think that's all we'll go into today," he said pleasantly, and I was dismissed.

The finger tremor that conspicuously appeared and led to the abrupt ending of the interview couldn't have come at a better time. If the captain had decided to probe deeply about my state of nerves, he might have learned that, although I was indeed healing, I had recently experienced one very severe dizzy spell. And this I did not want him to know of because I felt he was sick enough from listening to the troubles of his other patients.

The dizzy spell, incidentally, had been a real humdinger. It had occurred one evening as I was walking down a lit corridor just outside our ward. Suddenly the lights of the corridor spun around in my head. I was staggering, but I managed to make my way into the ward and get to my bed. It took several minutes for the spell to pass, but after it passed, I was none the worse for it, so there was no reason to mention it to him.

There was, I suppose, one serious flaw with my "no complaint strategy;" I didn't realize that psychiatry, too, had a strategy and theirs would turn out to be not quite so benign as mine.

It was, perhaps, in the late afternoon of the following day when I became disturbed by conversation of nearby patients in the ward.

"We wouldn't be here if it wasn't for those Jews," one of the patients was saying. "It's those damned Jews' fault!" And the other patients gathered around him were agreeing.

Listening to them slandering and knocking Jews, I started thinking of my loved ones. First of my sister, brother, and father, and then I started remembering my loving mother. Feeling totally helpless and in despair, I fell to crying, hiding my head under the bedsheets. Realizing I couldn't stop crying and aware that I didn't want others to know, I arose from the bed and went into the latrine where I cried my eyes out. While I was crying, a concerned attendant came up and asked me several times, "What's wrong, why are you crying?"

I didn't reply, just kept bawling like a baby. Finally, I cried everything out, and then feeling much better, I returned to my bed.

I didn't know what was happening to me. Why the return of these uncontrollable crying spells? Previous to my combat exhaustion, I had never once shed a tear about anything while in the Army. And I would have wondered about anyone who did. But previous to my combat exhaustion I had never had any reason to cry.

Having returned to my bed I wanted only to be left alone, so I hid myself under the sheets. And this time my mind, or rather my ears, picked up no outside conversation, but a thought or question related to my crying spell kept pounding in my head: "*Why! Why! Why do they hate us?*" Suddenly, out of nowhere, came the thought that I was suffering because I had been so unforgiving of my foster parents and their family. And then as I lay there thinking of them, I felt overcome by a feeling of forgiveness and then from the depth of my heart I forgave, I forgave them all.

Lying there hiding under the sheets, forgiving all, I suppose I should have felt a great sense of relief. Perhaps I did. I don't recall, because something else was bothering me. I was concerned about people I loved.

Alone and friendless with no one to turn to, I turned to God in prayer. And I prayed for a people I loved. And in answer to my prayer, words from my prayer book came to me, occupying my thought. These were words I'd paid little or no attention to previously, but words which now had meaning for me and comforted me. And the words that comforted me were, "And Israel arisen shall protect her own."

Evening came and I was feeling very good. Sitting up in bed, completely relaxed, at peace with the world, I was confronted by Captain Wilks. He had come over to me to ask me how I felt. And standing next to him was an attendant who'd informed him that I'd been crying.

Captain Wilks said nothing about this. He asked merely, "How are you feeling? Any problems?"

To his questions I answered truthfully that I felt fine. I didn't' stop to think that my eyes were still red from crying. Seemingly satisfied with my answers, he turned from me and, talking with the attendant, exited the ward. That was the last time I'd ever see Captain Wilks.

On the following morning an attendant came up to me and said, "Corporal Norber, you are to get your things together. You're being transferred to another ward."

Sitting in the ambulance that was transporting me to another ward, I had time to collect my thoughts. "Guess I'm going to the ward that gives passes to London." Recently, I heard that some patients, those who were getting along well, were transferred to a ward in which passes to London were made available. On hearing this, I had immediately written a letter to a girl I'd met in London in the spring of 1944. "Look for me soon," I'd written her.

After a brief spin the ambulance pulled over to a curb and stopped. The driver got out and opened the rear doors and then he led me up a concrete pathway that led to the front doors of my new ward. An attendant appeared and opened the doors of this ward and I stepped inside. Then I heard the keys locking the doors behind me. What I saw in front of me was unbelievable. Patients sitting in beds in catatonic positions, some with arms frozen over their heads, and others with their arms extended rigidly in front of them.

I stopped in my tracks, stunned.

"Move on, you miserable son-of-a-bitch!" The attendant, or rather, the guard shoved me onto a bed. "Stay there!" he commanded, and he walked off.

"Where am I, where am I?" I exclaimed.

I looked into the eyes of a seemingly sane and calm patient who had come over to my bed. He looked at me and all he said was, "You're in the asshole of creation."

ENVIRONMENTAL THERAPY*

Because of the terrorism that ruled this ward, I am unable to be certain as to the time sequence in which the events depicted occurred.

DAY ONE: It was a prisoner beating time, or rather, patient beating time. The patient in the bed next to me had defecated in bed, and as he sat staring blankly into space, a sadistic guard ran up and started pummeling him, beating him to a pulp. The helpless catatonic patient, on being beaten, shrieked and hooted like some wild animal. When the beating subsided and the animalistic shrieking stopped, a beat of a different sort took over: the flames, the moaning of burned men, then just flames, enveloped my mind. The nightmare images of the forest had returned to my mind and I was back in Hurtgen again.

We were in a basement and badly burned men lay moaning on the floor, dying alongside other severely wounded men. The infantry lieutenant nearby was talking to me.

"My men are having trouble identifying German tanks from American. Can you help?"

I took his field glasses from him and went up to the remains of the first floor. I was kneeling on a narrow ledge, behind part of a blown-down brick wall, looking through the field glasses, adjusting. A tank was milling around in the field.

"German tank, 200 yards!!"

At that instant the tank fired; the shell slammed into the bricks. The bricks flew, the field glasses flew, and I was in the basement being helped up by an infantryman.

Mortar which seconds before had held the bricks of the crumbling wall together was now sprayed and matted in my hair. My fingers became entangled when I tried to run them through my hair; pieces were also lodged in my throat. For days afterwards, whenever I contracted the muscles in my throat, I spat up bits of mortar which had become lodged in a hole in one of my tonsils. I spit the grimy bits of mortar out of my mouth, and walked back to report to the lieutenant. I was half in shock, he was composed and collected. We exchanged a few brief remarks and then he stood silently reviewing the situation. We had no anti-tank weapons of any sort left; the accompanying platoon of tanks and tank destroyers had been completely destroyed; we were low in ammunition and able-bodied men – in a matter of minutes our position could be easily overrun.

The lieutenant's firm voice carried throughout the basement: "Prepare to withdraw! Get the wounded ready. We'll load the half-tracks."

There were three half-tracks available. The badly wounded were loaded onto the first track. The walking wounded followed in the next vehicle. Ours was the last truck to move out. The withdrawal was orderly. And so we withdrew to more basements elsewhere along the line where our wounded could be attended to and hopefully sent to the rear, and we could regroup. Our platoon, or what was left of it, had shifted position, but Bergstein was still in our hands.

The shrieks and howling from the bed next to me snapped me back from Hurtgen to the harsh reality of the psycho ward I was in. The sadistic guard had resumed beating the helpless patient in the bed next to mine, and no other guard or attendant cared to stop it. Finally, the shrieking stopped and the patient slumped over, moaning in pain. And the moans of the men dying in the basements in Hurtgen faded in and out of my mind.

While all this was going on, there was a loudspeaker in our ward that was blaring on and on about some guy named Paul or Saul who was on the road to Damascus and had seen a light. What the message of Paul or Saul was, I couldn't understand, because a patient in front of me was being subdued by a guard who had him in a full nelson. "I am John the Baptist!" bellowed the patient as he struggled with his adversary, "I am John the Baptist!" He was being hustled to "Seclusion."

Day turned into night and I needed some sleeping pills. The horrifying images of burning men falling out of turrets gripped me. I rose from my bed, went past a napping attendant and entered the nurse's office.

"Could I please have some sleeping pills?" I asked her.

The nurse looked up and screamed for help. In response, an attendant rushed in and demanded to know what I was doing in this office. I said I wanted some sleeping pills. Seeing I meant no harm, the attendant calmed the nurse and turned to me, saying "Sorry, no pills." Then he led me from the office back to bed.

It was some time in the middle of the night and I was in the middle of a wide-awake nightmare. This time I approached the attendant who had led me from the nurse's office earlier. "Could I have a piece of paper, an envelope, and a pencil?" I asked.

"Okay," he said, and he got up and got me what I asked for.

By a dim light near my bed I wrote to Captain Wilks, begging him to please come immediately to get me out of this ward. I signed my brief "Ze

Stray Saint Louis Kid." I was now out of my mind and suffering from paranoiac delusions.

I handed the envelope addressed to "Capt. Wilks", no address given, to the attendant and asked him to be sure to see that Captain Wilks got it. He nodded.

I didn't sleep at all that night, so when morning came I felt completely washed out. The paranoiac episode had passed and somehow I knew Captain Wilks would not appear to rescue me.

"Captain Patterson wants to see you in his office." The attendant bringing these glad tidings ushered me into the doctor's office and left immediately, shutting the door behind him.

Captain Patterson sat at his desk. He looked at me with something like amusement showing in his eyes. Was it a smirk or smile? I didn't know.

I saluted. He returned my salute.

"Empty your pockets," he commanded. "Put everything on my desk."

I put my prayer book and the picture of Christ on his desk. He looked at the objects on his desk and then at me. He said nothing, just studied me.

"Sit down," he commanded.

I sat. If he'd said, "Bark," I would've barked. I was unbelievably afraid of this man. After what I'd seen in his ward, I had good reason to fear him.

"I want to ask you some questions," he said, drawing my chart from his desk drawer, placing it before him. "Hmmmm, a tank gunner, you were a tank gunner?"

"Yes, sir."

"Were you always a tank gunner?"

"No, sir, once I was a tank commander, in a battle, but Captain Pool didn't know about that."

"You read this sheet of paper I'm holding in my hands?"

"Yes, sir."

He stared at me and I stared back. I had to my knowledge done nothing wrong.

"Where did you come from before you came to this ward?" he asked.

"Captain Wilks," I said.

"What hospital?" he pressed.

"I don't know, I just know I came from Captain Wilks."

He resumed reading my record. "Hmmm, you lived in a foster home?"

"Yes, sir."

Captain Patterson wasted no time in getting to the point he had in mind: "Did you like the people you lived with?"

"No, sir."

"You disliked them intensely?"

"Yes, sir."

"You hated them," he said, stressing the word "hated."

Again I replied, simply, "Yessir."

"Did they ever hit you?" he asked.

"No, sir."

"But you hated them."

"Yes, sir."

In response Captain Patterson sat silently, saying nothing, just staring at me. Finally, "Did you forgive them?"

"Yes, sir," I replied. (Had this question been asked of me in any previous psychiatric interview, my answer would have been "No".)

Again the captain sat staring at me, saying nothing; and then for the first time in the interview I thought I detected a light behind his eyes. A light of approval.

Now my doctor went on to other matters. He wanted to know about my mating instincts and sex life. After a brief interrogation, in which he learned I was a normal heterosexual, he ended the mental part of my examination.

My office visit was concluded with a brief physical exam. And after that it was back to the ward.

Things in the menagerie were pretty much the same as they had been the day before, with a few variations. "John the Baptist" strolled by my bed. He was out of the full-nelson, but in a straitjacket. The poor catatonic in the bed next to me was again receiving a beating for defecating in bed. His tormentor, now registered in my mind as The Evil One, was the same bullying, sadistic guard who had beaten him senseless the previous day. The atmosphere in the ward was foul and malevolent.

Now a new commotion started in the center of the room. A newcomer had entered our nest of hell. For a moment the bullying, sadistic guard's attention was drawn from the defecator to the new prey, a battle-fatigued paratrooper. The Evil One went to greet him.

In no time he had the demoralized paratrooper groveling on the floor before him, cowering and pleading with the guard not to do him in. All was normal. Evil ruled supreme.

Anyhow, for the next four or five "normal" days I managed to survive endless nightmares and sickening days without incurring the wrath of the vile guard. Then one evening he came up to my bed and started cursing me and threatening me. Another attendant intervened on my behalf, telling him, "Let him alone, he doesn't bother anybody." The Evil One backed off, but in his mind he knew he'd find a way.

Perhaps later that night or the night following, I had to go to the latrine. Since the latrine was locked and "patients" had to be accompanied by an attendant to be allowed entrance, I had to ask an attendant to accompany me into the latrine. Unfortunately, he turned me over to the

Evil One. I'll never forget the ordeal. Just the two of us in that locked latrine; I had to beg and plead for the toilet paper.

Shortly afterwards, I was in bed and the inerasable images of the flames of burning men resumed haunting me. I felt engulfed by the flames, and not realizing what I was doing, I strayed from my bed too far. And then I saw him, the Evil One, lunge for me. I dove out of his way, but in so doing, I tripped or fell, striking my crazy bone on the sharp edge of my bed frame. A loud bonging sound, like a gong being struck, started up in my head, and my face felt a paralyzing grip spreading over it, and I passed into merciful sleep. And this very special hell would have to wait until morning before it could again besiege me.

NOTES FROM A MEDICAL ATMOSPHERE

A day or so later, I was transferred from Captain Patterson's snake pit to the insulin ward of Captain Dorsey, where I would undergo deep insulin shock treatment. In this form of shock treatment, measured amounts of insulin are injected into the patient's veins until the patient begins to perspire profusely and falls into a coma.

So there I was, lying on a clean hospital bed, in clean sheets on a rubber protected mattress, sweating like hell. I was spread-eagled with my wrists and ankles bound to the bed.

"Why do you always tie my wrists and ankles to the bed? I'm not going anywhere."

"That's so you won't flail and hurt yourself when you go into coma."

"But I've taken several treatments and I have yet to go into a coma."

"You will, you will."

And so it went until my first coma came after a week or so of treatments.

"Nurse, there's a pumping in my head. What's the pumping in my head? And what's the swishing in my head?"

"Your brain is being rinsed."

"You know, nurse, every day just prior to my going into a coma I see twenty-five little, no, not so little white configurations that appear in a definite sequence. What are these configurations?"

"Forget these configurations. You're not really conscious when you see them."

"Well, if I'm not conscious, how come I see them now as I'm talking to you and I know what we're talking about?"

"Forget it, Norber. Forget it."

But I couldn't forget it. Too many strange things were going on inside my head and I couldn't ignore these things. For a period of perhaps two to six weeks I was forced to take the treatments.

When at last it became apparent to the doctor that the results were anything but good, he ordered the treatments discontinued. Of course, by this time I had a rinsed, drained, sprained brain that was sitting atop a body with a worn out central nervous system. And in that condition, while sitting on a bed weeping, an attendant dropped by my bed to tell me

Captain Dorsey had arranged passage for me on a hospital ship that was going back to the States in the morning.

(Nine years later a prominent neuro-psychiatrist, treating me for a condition in which my spinal fluid manufactured too fast for bodily absorption, questioned me as to whether I had ever had the strange symptoms that were affecting me at the time. Pointedly, he asked me, "Did you ever before hear this gonging in your head? Have you ever had any of these symptoms before?" And I, being afraid of all psychiatrists, lied and said no.)

Thank God the treatment of the battle fatigued veterans is vastly improved, so I'm told. Battle fatigue is no longer a stigma. Psychiatrists no longer applaud generals who slap battle fatigue cases.

THE JOURNEY BACK TO SANITY

There was no sunlight in the hold of the hospital ship that was transporting us psychos back to the States. In a locked up section below deck, inhaling stale air and cigarette smoke may not be traveling first class, but considering the fact that no one was mistreated or threatened in any way, there was little most of us cared to complain about.

We, the cargo, were a subdued group. Most of us suffered from extreme feelings of guilt and worthlessness, and I believe, most of us felt like scum. One guilt-ridden lieutenant attempted suicide, but was discovered before he succeeded in hanging himself. (He spent the entire homeward cruise behind bars in his birthday suit.) If any one of us doubted for a moment that he was crazy, all he had to do was read his name tag that was tied to a belt loop on his pants. For following our name, there appeared the Latin or Greek name of the disease that afflicted us. According to our tags, most of us were dementia something or schizophrenic something. I spent most of our journey wondering what the hell kind of kook I really was.

The best part of our journey was the ending. I'll never forget what happened at the dock in Charleston, South Carolina; and I'll never

171

remember it, either. That's what kind of a memorable blur I walked around in on realizing I was back home in America.

One thing I remember rather clearly was walking down the gangplank wondering about dementia praecox, catatonia, hebephrenic, and the rest of the "self-explanatory" terms I'd been exposed to. And the next thing I remember was driving in a bus convoy with my Greek and Latin-minded comrades.

And the last thing I remember was unloading from the buses and assembling in some sort of formations on a field in front of "The Stark General Hospital," the Army hospital in Charleston, South Carolina.

I was standing in a long line waiting to see a psychiatrist who stood at the head of the line, and whose duty it was to determine in a one-minute interview or less just how nutty each of us in the line might be. Those who failed to impress the doctor favorably were to be sent to closed wards. Those who could hold up under the strain of a one minute interview without cracking passed and were sent to "open." I passed.

My exam had been rather simple. The doctor looked me in the eye and asked me one question: "Are you hearing any voices?" And I said, "No, sir, just yours."

For two or three days I was on my own. Once again, I was allowed freedom in a hospital. I dined in the main mess hall of the hospital and was allowed to be off-ward certain hours of the day. Had I been well, I would've enjoyed these privileges. Unfortunately, I was so sick I couldn't know the meaning of enjoyment.

My shipping orders came through on about the third day after my arrival at Stark, and this time I was notified I was being sent to Colorado.

On a spring-like morning in 1945, probably April or May, I walked into a sleeper coach of the train that was to take me to Colorado. A lower berth was open for me and waiting. I knew it was my berth because the soldier who accompanied me into the coach told me it was my berth. He also told me to remove all my clothes and get into a pair of pajamas he was handing me. I was confused and thought is unusual that I should be forced to travel across country, from South Carolina to Colorado, in pajamas, but there was nothing I could do about it. The soldier who accompanied me was a decent sort. He explained to me in clipped, yet courteous terms, that he was merely following orders and I had to do likewise.

After getting into my pajamas, I drew back the curtains to my berth and looked around. The coach was completely empty. I glanced outside my window. There stood the soldier at the entrance to the coach. He was on guard.

The trip across country to Colorado was uneventful. When we reached our destination the guard returned my clothes to me and told me we were in Colorado Springs, Colorado, and I was being sent to the hospital in Camp Carson.

Shortly afterwards, I was sitting in a reception ward in Camp Carson Hospital waiting for a psychiatrist to see me. Other new arrivals were also sitting around waiting to be called.

A man in white was tapping me on my shoulder. "Are you Corporal Norber?"

"Yes, I am," I replied, "but sometimes I wish I wasn't!"

"Follow me, please."

The door to the doctor's room was open and we walked right in. The doctor motioned the attendant to leave; he left, shutting the door behind him, leaving me facing the doctor.

My doctor this time was a Chinese woman, an Army officer, who sat at her desk holding a dictaphone in her hand.

There'll be no errors this time, I thought. I know all about dictaphones. She'll probably repeat things I say, so if she gets anything wrong I'll correct her immediately. I knew all about dictaphones, but I didn't know my Chinese psychiatrist. I didn't know she'd put words in my mouth.

At a nod and the words, "Be Seated," I sat.

"What day of week this is?" she asked.

"I don't know."

"Can you tell me the month, date and year this is?"

"It's 1945," I said, answering the last part of the question first.

"And the month and date?"

This stumped me, so I started muttering, trying to figure out the month. "Let's see now. I know I left the front around Christmas or New Years..."

"You will please tell me month and date it is now!" she demanded.

"If you'll wait just a minute or so I'll figure it out."

She waited.

To myself I started figuring and counting on my fingers. First there was Captain Wilks' ward, maybe a week or two, then Captain Patterson's snake pit, again a week or two. From there I was put in the insulin ward of Captain Dorsey, where I underwent deep insulin shock therapy. How many times had I been in a coma; or how many weeks? Was it a month or two? God, my mind is blurry.

"You will please tell me the month and date," she persisted.

"Uh, uh, it's March," and then allowing more time for the insulin ward, "or April"; then realizing it appeared to be springtime outside, I added, "or May."

She summarized what I had said beautifully. "It's March, April or May. Which month you choose?"

I chose one.

Not indicating to me whether I'd hit the right month or not, she asked, "And the date?"

I chose any number from one to thirty.

Now she relayed to her dictaphone my choices for month and date, while I sat in a quandry wondering how the hell I should know the month and date.

176

Having concluded the time orientation part of my interrogation, my doctor turned to sex, the psychiatrist's favorite subject. "You like girls?"

And so we discussed my favorite subject.

My answers to her questions were all within the range of normalcy, so we proceeded rapidly to the one subject that soon appeared to be uppermost in her mind – the subject of VOICES.

Staring at me intently, she asked, "Have you ever heard a voice when no one is present?"

"Yes," I said, "I have."

"How many times you hear voice?"

"Once," I replied.

"What did the voice say to you?"

"You wouldn't understand," I replied, and shook my head.

"Voice say 'You wouldn't understand'?" she asked.

"No," I said, "I just said *YOU* wouldn't understand about the voice."

"What did the voice say to you?" She repeated her question.

This time I answered her directly. "The voice said, 'Go back on earth, your time is not over.'"

She spoke into her dictaphone. "Voice say 'Go back on earth, your time is not over yet.'"

"I didn't say 'yet,'" I corrected.

"Yes, you did," she replied. "You said 'not yet over'."

"Well, which is it; did I say *'YET OVER' or 'OVER YET?'*"

There followed one or two minutes of arguing about 'yet,' 'yet over,' and 'over yet,' until I wasn't sure myself if the voice had used the word 'yet.' Finally, I gave up and agreed I said whatever she said I said.

Her next question: "Whose voice was it spoke to you?"

"I don't know," I answered.

"Whose voice you think it was; you must have idea voice belong to somebody."

"No, I have no idea who the voice belonged to."

She pressed further. "You think God talked to you?"

"No, I didn't say that."

"Well, who did you think talked to you?"

"I don't know, I don't know what to think; I didn't know what to think; I didn't think and I don't think!"

Following this outburst there followed another argument; this time on what I think. Finally, after defending my thought processes or lack of them as best I could, I conceded in exasperation, "Okay, have it your way, I think God spoke to me!"

Satisfied, she addressed her dictaphone, "Patient say God spoke to him."

I never thought that! She insisted, so..

She sat staring through me, thinking long, I supposed, about how she would phrase her next questions. I felt I knew what was coming; under what circumstances did the voice come to you. But, no, I was wrong. She was only interested in voices, plural.

"You ever hear other voices?"

"Well, certainly," I replied. "Every time someone speaks to me I hear a voice. I hear your voice now, as I sit here in this room with you."

"You know what I mean," she said. "When no one in room with you. You know what I mean, you hear a voice, and you do not know who spoke?"

"No," I said simply.

For reasons completely unknown to me, she refused to accept my simple answer. So she repeated herself.

"I ask you again, you ever hear any other voice speak to you, not know who voice belong to? I mean when no one in room?"

"Whew," I sighed, "I guess I might as well confess. Yes, yes, I heard another voice when I was alone in a room. Yes, I heard a voice."

She leaned forward. "What did the voice say?"

"This is K.O.A.," I replied, sounding like a radio announcer.

"Oho, you make big joke," she said indignantly.

I was worn out, and being slightly manic, I started to laugh. This disturbed her. It disturbed her very much. As a matter of fact, she got so disturbed I got locked up.

Inside a large, vacant, locked ward stood two attendants, one on each side of me. They were asking me to relinquish custody of my razor blades and shoe strings. I started to protest, to argue that I could be trusted. They turned a deaf ear on me. When I saw it was useless to protest, I yielded.

For several days I slumped in a seclusion room off this large, almost empty ward. There was one other patient assigned to this ward, and he was so sick it was painful just to look at him. All day long he walked around the ward saying nothing, just twitching.

One day I awoke to find a newspaper on my bed. The headlines screamed the glorious news: "GERMANY SURRENDERS!" I was too sick to feel anything. That is, anything but dejection. I got up and went for a walk in the hallway outside my room. Several psychiatrists entered the hallway; one walked up to me and said, "Have you heard the latest? We've won in Europe!"

"I oughta be shot," I said.

The psychiatrist appeared startled. He looked at me like I was crazy.

"Why do you say that?" he asked.

"Because I'm a coward."

Despite the fact that he was an officer in the United States Army of America, he did not look at me with disdain. Instead he said simply, "Here we don't distinguish between heroes and cowards." Then he left me alone to ponder that one.

A day or so later an officer, perhaps the same one I'd encountered in the hallway, entered my seclusion room to tell me I was being transferred to a hospital in Denver and that I'd probably be assigned to a locked ward there The man was straight-forward. I knew after speaking with him I'd not be dumped in a violent ward and left to rot.

FITZSIMONS

(Not So Rocky in the Rockies)

The doctor who greeted me on my arrival at Fitzsimons General Hospital in Denver did not lie or play games with me. He did not sit behind a desk and wait for me to be locked up in his ward. Instead, he met the ambulance that had transported me from Camp Carson to his doorstep. We met outside his ward near a recreational ball diamond. After introducing himself as "Doctor Sherry" (he was a civilian), he quickly told me that I was assigned to his ward; that it was a locked ward; that he knew I was very tired of being in locked wards; that "they" at Fitzsimons wanted to help me heal, and he concluded his opening spiel by stating when I showed signs of healing, I'd be transferred to an open ward.

I expressed doubt that I could ever heal in any way in a locked ward. I also told him it was difficult for me to understand how he, a civilian, could be in charge of anything at a military hospital.

He responded that he was retained by the government as a doctor on a psychiatric staff that was headed by Major Barbato. As for the locked ward, he emphasized again that he was well aware of my feelings, but that they felt it would be better for me to be assigned to a locked ward at this time.

I glanced at the ambulance driver who was standing nearby. I had no thought of running away. Where could I go? I knew I really had no choice. Reluctantly, in a depressed state, I followed the doctor into the ward. As the doors closed behind us, I felt within me a sense of utter hopelessness.

Despite the sudden straight-forwardness I was now encountering in psychiatrists, I could not like them as a group, because they too often had been deceitful and dishonest in dealing with me. The stench of Captain Patterson's foul pit still remained with me. The rotten treatment I'd received there, I felt certain, was nowhere revealed in my record. The locked insulin ward which followed had been an improvement, true, but the results of the intravenous insulin treatments had been horrendous. (Following the treatments I was completely broken and I bore no resemblance whatsoever to the man I once thought myself to be.) The locked ward holdover at Carson, while not bad, had only served to maintain my sense of worthlessness.

So what was to be accomplished in my being locked up at Fitszimsons? I wondered.

"Why am I kept locked up like this? I've done nothing to you people."

A cheerful darling little brunette nurse was listening to me plead for my freedom.

"You'll like it here," the pretty little one was saying, as if my new quarters were a palace. "We have movies two or three times a week and every afternoon we have a Coke break. Look around, do the patients around here seem unhappy?"

I looked around. The ward was indeed a nice place, light and airy, and the patients appeared to be rational and friendly people. And they were at ease, some sitting on their beds reading books, while others were playing cards. And milling about the ward were several cheerful nurses and attendants. The pleasantness of the atmosphere was unlike anything I had ever known in any previous lock-up.

"Where are your strait-jackets hidden?"

"If you're going to talk like that, I'm not going to talk to you!" Then she added reassuringly, "You'll see, this is not a bad place. You'll get adjusted."

Much later, before retiring, I learned that two of my fellow patients had been survivors of the Bataan Death March and had spent over two years as prisoners of the Japanese. Then I understood the absence of surly guards and straight-jackets.

In the early evening of my second day on the ward, an attendant came to my bed to tell me I had a visitor waiting to see me. Since I'd been completely out of touch with all my family and friends for several months, and I was unaware of visitors being allowed to see patients, I asked the attendant who my visitor might be. He responded to my question, saying, "Just follow me." And with that he led me through the ward's locked doors into a hallway. Immediately to my left was a small waiting room. When the attendant opened the door to this room I saw seated before me a smiling corporal who bore a family resemblance to me.

"Ted!" I blurted, "where did you come from? How did you know I'm here???!"

The shock of seeing my brother whom I hadn't seen in three long years suddenly materialized as if out of nowhere momentarily brought me out of my doldrums and sharpened my senses. Seating myself on a chair opposite my brother, I quickly learned that he was stationed at Fort Warren, an Army camp a hundred miles away. And, he said, earlier in the afternoon the Army notified him that I was at Fitzsimons and was allowed to have visitors. Minutes later, he had an emergency pass in his hands and was on his way here.

Having explained his presence, he then asked how things had been going my way.

Eftsoons, I launched into a tale of horror, describing hellish scenes from a battlefield. And during the battle, I muttered my prayers. And after the battle, I gave thanks unto God for having delivered me. All this, brother Ted, an avowed atheist, heard as he sat spellbound, held prisoner by the "glittering eye" of a battle fatigued soldier. At least that's the way brother Ted described our meeting that memorable day, comparing me to The Ancient Mariner.

Though I may be somewhat hazy in remembering my end of the conversation, I remember quite well what brother Ted had to say about grace and thanks. "I got here long after visiting hours were over, and it's only through the grace of the good psychiatrist who heads your section, a Major Barbato, that I was allowed in to see you. Thanks unto him."

I must have said something about my feelings for psychiatrists in general, because the next thing I knew my brother was singing the praises of not only this one good psychiatrist, he mentioned, but all psychiatrists in general. "They know what they're doing. They're scientists, doctors of the mind. You're in good hands!"

And so it went, this most unusual disagreement. Brother Ted, the atheist, hearing me praising God, and I, who had spent time in a psychiatric snake-pit, hearing him praising psychiatrists.

Whatever else Ted and I discussed in his first visit was not too well remembered by me. One important thing, I do remember, however, is hearing that my sister Irma was coming to Denver to join Ted and they would both be visiting me on the following day. This was particularly welcome and refreshing news for me to hear. For though I idolized my brother and was very happy to see him, my sister was the one member of the family in whom I confided. This, of course, had come about quite naturally as a consequence of our having grown up together in a foster home.

When the separation of our family had occurred late in 1932 following our mother's death, my sister and I were placed by a children's bureau in a foster home. At the time I had just turned twelve and Irma was approaching or had just reached her fourteenth birthday.

The memory of that bleak wintry day our family dissolved would forever be indelibly imprinted in my mind. I was in school, sitting at my desk in a classroom, when my teacher approached and asked me to please step out into the hallway with her. On entering the hall, I was startled to see my father. Soon I was hearing dreaded words; my father and my teacher were both explaining to me that I was leaving this school and transferring to another because I was going to live elsewhere, in another home, a foster home, a home of strangers. I started to protest. "But I don't want to live with strangers; I don't want to live elsewhere! I like this school and I like my home!" But my protests were of no avail.

A children's bureau had somehow entered the picture of our family's life and this bureau had arranged for my sister and me to be sent to a foster home. My sister and I had never been told one word about this or asked what our feelings might be about leaving our home. We were just told we were going. And that was that.

Our family, weakened by my Mom's death, and a father who had become destitute, simply couldn't survive as a unit.

In the hallway of that public grammar school, I was getting my first real taste of what life was really all about if one were penniless. The only bit of comforting news I heard in the hallway were my father's soothing words telling me that my sister and I would be together in our foster home, while he and my brother were going to live in our aunt's home which was located only a few blocks from the foster home. Irma and I could visit them, I was assured, whenever we wished. Since the bureau's only other available placement was the orphan's home, it appeared that the best arrangements had been made that could have been made for our family.

Without placing blame on anyone in any quarters, the foster home we entered was a disaster area. My sister and I simply couldn't co-exist with our foster parents and their family. The adolescent years can be troublesome for natural parents with their offspring, let alone foster parents, but in our case, the conflicts that grew between them and us became irremediable. For a period of five and a half years my sister and I lived in an environment seething with hatred. At no time did we complain to the children's bureau because we lived in constant fear that we would be separated and sent to an orphan's home.

Living under the same roof, drinking the same cup of bitterness and hoping against hope for the day of deliverance when our own family would be reunited, my sister and I existed. In this setting the relationship that grew and developed between Irma and me was one that was totally devoid of sibling rivalry.

In the summer of 1938, Irma, who was now self-supporting, made arrangements for us to leave the foster home. The two of us separated, each of us going to live with different relatives. Our dreams of having our own home had faded and died by then, but the strong bond that had grown between my sister and me remained.

The pretty red-haired girl sitting opposite me in the visitor's room was asking me some personal questions about my plans for the future and if my plans included marriage. My pretty red-haired questioner was my sister, Irma. I did not fear her or her questions.

"And do you plan to return to St. Louis when you get out of here, that is, out of the Army?"

"I have no plans. I just want OUT!!! I can go anywhere: Denver, St. Louis, anywhere, I just want out!!!"

"And the girl back East; do you perhaps think of going back there and getting married?"

"No way," I responded suddenly, thinking of the beauty I knew I'd never see again. "No way, I'll just jump out of a psycho ward into marriage."

Irma thought a moment, reflecting on my well-worded reply. Perhaps she reflected on her own brief marriage. She, herself, had only recently divorced her husband after a marriage that had lasted only three or four years. Had she thought what she was doing when she jumped into marriage?

"You're sure," she persisted, "that in the back of your mind you're not thinking of running back East and looking up your girlfriend?"

"Yes, I'm sure; I'm absolutely certain. I'm not ready for marriage at this time. Besides, I really think it would be best for me to return to St. Louis when I leave here so I could maybe get my bearings."

Irma seemed much relieved. I was making sense. A lot of sense, considering my present status.

Satisfied that I wouldn't go from a psycho ward into marriage, my sister decided to tell me some important news she had delayed telling me.

"Since we've been out of touch so long, there's something I've got to bring you up to date on about my marriage. It's over. I divorced him." And then she explained briefly that her marriage had been a very unhappy experience and the most fortunate thing that could be said about it was that it had been childless. Because of that, her divorce had been uncomplicated and a new start on life was made much easier for her. She spoke with no bitterness about her marriage and it was evident she was very happy to be single again.

In updating me on other conditions on the home front, she told me that Dad was working hard and doing well in the real estate business. He couldn't make the trip to Fitzsimons with her because he had a severe spring cold, she explained, but he wanted her to let me know he was now financially well off and was planning to reestablish our household. And she emphasized that more than anything else in this world he wanted to see all of us living together as a family again.

My response to Dad's suggestion that I return home was guarded. "We're not children anymore," I said. "Ted's thirty, you're twenty-six, and I'm twenty-four. If the war with Japan ended tomorrow, and we were all home the day after that, how long would we all be together before wedding bells break up 'that old gang of ours?'"

"No matter for how long," Irma replied. "I think it would be great if we could all live together, however briefly, under one roof as a family once more."

Ted, who was seated next to Irma, spoke up. "What Irma is saying is not only would it be good for all of us seated here to touch home base again, but it would be good for Dad, too. You've got to realize that Dad was deprived of his family because of hard times. He missed his family. Now, because of the war, business times are good and Dad has come along with these times. He's bounced back. And the greatest pleasure he could imagine would be to have his family back together with him; until we get married, that is."

It was truly amazing for me to hear these good things from my sister and brother about our father. In my growing up years, while living in the foster home, I had come to think of Dad as a very poor man who couldn't keep his family together. I saw him as an abject failure, weak and powerless. Though I loved him dearly, I was also ashamed of him. Never mind the Great Depression or the devastating effect of Mom's death must have had on him, and never mind that he was an immigrant, with no formal schooling, who had maintained his family and made his way in the business world prior to the Depression. These things, as a child, I never saw or reckoned with. So now it was difficult for me to see Dad as a successful businessman.

Had I been well, everything Irma and Ted had been telling me would have made sense to me. But I wasn't well. Long months of confinement had made me sick and my reaction to everything I was hearing was inappropriate. Forgetting for the moment what I'd said about returning to St. Louis, I suddenly erupted. *"I want out now, and I mean now! I don't care where I go. I want out!!!"*

While I was harping on this one note, my keeper in a white coat, came over to us. Visiting hours were over.

On the following day, Sunday, our final meeting took place. With the doctor's approval, I was permitted to leave the building and walk around outside with my visitors. Walking around the ball diamond with my brother and sister gave me a sense of openness and freedom I hadn't experienced in quite some time. True, an attendant had accompanied us outside, but he kept a respectful distance away from us and I felt my conversation with Irma and Ted was not being overheard.

Our conversation picked up where it had left off the previous day. We again spoke of home and the future, and suddenly one important subject popped up: education.

Ted had asked if I had any plans to return to school under a government educational bill for ex-servicemen.

My addled mind responded that I had never heard of such a bill for ex-servicemen. Was my brother sure there was such a bill?

"You do know the war with Germany is over?" he asked kiddingly. I listened intently as my brother then explained how, under the provisions of this bill, I would be eligible to get a free college education. And I continued listening intently as my brother outlined a plan for my future. "You know, you're still young and you could go to Washington University and get an all-expense free education. And on top of that, you could have the added security of living at home while you're getting this education."

At this time when the only things that gripped my mind were getting out and getting a girl in my arms, my brother had to bring up college. Now I had something else to think about.

Imagine, going back to school, going to college, tuition paid.

If nothing else, this final visit with my brother and sister opened my eyes to the possibility of a brighter tomorrow.

At the close of our visit Irma said to me, "Then it's settled. I'll tell Dad you're planning to stay single for a while, anyhow, and you'll be returning to St. Louis when you get out of the Army. And one last thing: I promise you, Vic, when you arrive in St. Louis, your home, our home, we'll be waiting for you."

No one ever had a sweeter sister than I.

OCCUPATIONAL THERAPY

According to Doc Sherry, the dictionary was right in defining occupational therapy as the treatment of nervous, mental or physical disabilities by means of work adapted to favor recovery and normal readjustment to external conditions. Also, according to Doc Sherry, occupational therapy, otherwise known as O.T., was the most effective type of therapy used in the healing process of his patients.

At least I got this impression when I spoke to the doctor requesting that I be allowed to be excused from taking occupational therapy.

Our conversation had gone something like this:

"Why do you want to be excused from occupational therapy?"

"Because I'm terrible at making wallets and belts. I'm terrible working with my hands. Even when I was in grammar school I was a failure in arts and crafts and manual training."

"It's good for you!"

"What's good for me?"

"O.T. – Occupational Therapy. Isn't that what we're talking about? It's good for you, it's therapy!"

"So are softball and volleyball. Don't you call that recreational therapy? I'd sure appreciate it if you would substitute some of the recreational therapy in place of occupational therapy."

The portly doctor was starting to get red in the face. "In no way are you going to be excused from O.T. O.T. is the centerpiece in our program for your healing and in no way are you going to be excused from it, and that's final!

My courteous and rational approach to a perplexing problem had been rudely rejected.

Having no option in the matter, I reluctantly attended all O.T. classes, which incidentally were scheduled on a daily basis. Of course, being inadequate at arts and crafts, I spent my time in class watching the other patients making wallets and belts. I was a spectator. Pleasant and quiet, I gave nobody any trouble in the classroom. When I was reproached at times by the instructor or an attendant for not actively engaging in the making of leather articles, I always pointed out that I could only do what I could do.

On the day Doc Sherry barged into our ward and descended upon me with a note in his hand and an unreasonable look in his eyes, I knew I was in for trouble.

"I've been informed," he glared, "that you refuse to do any work of any sort in the occupational therapy room."

"You have been informed correctly," I informed him. And then in defense of myself, I again told him of my ineptitudes in the field of arts and crafts and wallet making.

Doctor Sherry countered this by suggesting that perhaps I could find occupational therapy more acceptable if I started working with tools and mechanical objects.

I rejected this suggestion, saying I was not mechanically inclined.

At this, Doc Sherry became incensed with me. Suddenly, he lost control of himself. Throwing up his arms in exasperation, he shrieked, "There must be something you'd like to take apart and put back together again!"

I responded evenly and coolly, "Yes, doctor, there is. Do you have any machine guns? I'd prefer the Browning 30 Caliber Machine Gun Model M-1 A-4, heavy barrel, air-cooled, belt fed." But the doctor wasn't listening. He was exiting the ward in nothing flat.

I had been square with the doctor in pointing to guns as mechanical objects I liked to take apart and put back together again. As a former tank gunner I'd spent a great deal of time detail stripping and cleaning and reassembling the 30 and 50 caliber machine guns on my tank as well as the 75mm. Were it not for my understanding of the functioning of guns, I could have been classified as a complete mechanical illiterate. I was one of the finest tank gunners in the U.S. armored forces because I was well-coordinated and not because I was mechanically inclined.

So it wasn't my fault the doctor didn't take these things into consideration when we chatted. And it certainly wasn't my fault that the occupational therapy room didn't have up-to-date equipment.

On the day following my confrontation with the doctor, my brother showed up in the visitor's room with a puzzled look on his face. "Doctor Sherry just gave me a message for you and I don't know what it means. He said I should tell you to quit pulling his leg. When I asked him what he meant by that, he said 'Your brother can tell you.' So tell me, what's it all about?"

I was as perplexed as my brother, so I said I had no idea what he was talking about.

The confusion was cleared up for me at the start of the new week when an attendant came to me to inform me my presence would no longer be required in the occupational therapy class. "Doc Sherry likes your humor," he said.

"What humor??" I asked.

The attendant leaned toward me with a maniacal gleam in his eye. "Got any guns, Doc?"

GEORGE....I THINK

On a beautiful summery day in late June I was sitting on a bench located in a hall outside the staff room. Inside the staff room sat the review board, a medical group which would soon interview and observe me and decide if I were well enough to be transferred to an open ward.

I was sitting on this bench going over in my mind the questions I felt sure would be asked of me: "What do you plan to do when you are discharged from this hospital, and what are your plans for the future?" And I'd reply that I planned to return to St. Louis, that I'd live at home with my sister and father, and that after a brief period of adjustment I would return to school, taking advantage of the GI Bill (the new educational bill.)

I could picture myself acting like a sane and sensible person and I could see the board, seeing that I was sane and sensible, nodding their heads in agreement that I should be transferred from the locked ward to an open ward immediately.

Seated next to me on this bench in the hallway was a patient whose face was familiar, but whose name I didn't know. So, in starting up a conversation with him, I first said, "Your face is familiar, but I can't seem to recall your name."

To this he replied hesitantly, "George, I think."

I noticed he had a look of uncertainty, but that didn't stop me from trying to be sociable. "Well, where are you from?" I asked.

He hesitated. "One of the Dakotas, I think."

Now the blank yet anxious look made sense. His problem was obvious. He had some sort of amnesia. So I changed the subject and started talking about things like the weather and how pretty the nurses were. Our conversation didn't last long because an attendant interrupted us and asked George to accompany him into the staff room. I felt a little sorry for "George, I think," because he obviously was not in good shape. Yet, despite my sympathy, I realized that following him I should look good. Not only did I know my name, rank and serial number, but in addition, I could sound intelligent.

When my turn came, I sat in the staff room and handled all the questions the staff threw at me in an alert and intelligent manner. At the conclusion of the interview, I left the room with a feeling of strength and buoyancy. I didn't believe, like some psychos I'd known, that I'd been a sensational hit, but rather I felt certain my interview would lead to my immediate transfer to an open ward, or possibly even an immediate discharge.

Several days later I was standing in the middle of my ward talking with "George, I think," who'd come into our ward earlier in the day. George's condition hadn't improved, and I was wondering what he was doing in our ward. We had just exchanged greetings when we were interrupted by an attendant who told George to get his things together, that he was being discharged. A member of his family had come for him.

When I heard this, I said to the attendant, "Hey, what about me? I went before the staff, too!"

The attendant grinned knowingly. "Yeah, I heard about that."

After George had departed, I learned from the attendant that some patients in poor condition were discharged from the hospital if the staff felt further hospitalization would not benefit the patient. In many of these cases, I was told a member of the patient's family had to come in for him, and the patient was released in that person's custody. In George's particular case, I don't remember who the attendant said that person was. But it was probably his brother, I think.

BILL

Several days had passed since I had appeared before the board, and it appeared to me that no action had been taken on my case. I was still firmly entrenched in the locked ward.

Sitting on my bed, in a depressed mood, my thoughts were interrupted by a mail clerk who handed me a small manila envelope. "This beat-up envelope just got to our mailroom," he said, "and it's falling apart, so I thought I'd take a break and hand deliver it to you."

I took the jagged, torn, half-opened envelope from him and handled it carefully. It had been torn and scotch-taped, in so many places and had so many forwarding addresses written across it, it looked like it had gone through half the post offices in the U.S. Army. I looked at the return address: Co. B., 10th Tank Bn, A.P.O. 255.

On opening the envelope, I found a small booklet autographed by the officers and men of my company and accompanying the booklet was a letter. I was elated to hear from my outfit. I opened the booklet and thumbed through the pages looking at the signatures, then set it aside and picked up the letter. The first part of the letter was heartwarming, the writer letting me know I had a lot of friends. They hadn't forgotten me. I was enjoying myself immensely reading all about my friends. I was very happy reading the news until I came to the line. "And Bill Aldy was killed in the battle." I dropped the letter on the bed and it came to rest on an opened page of the autographed booklet. One signature stared back at me, that of T/4 Willie Aldy (Bill).

My thoughts turned back to seeing Bill for the last time. It was in December of '44 and I was standing in the hallway of the two-story frame house staring out the window at the beautiful snow-blanketed trees that glistened in a starry Christmas-like night, and Bill had asked, "Will you write my mother for me, Vic?" Bill looked very tired and worn then. He'd survived Hurtgen and this had been his one request.

"Yes," I remembered replying, "a little later." But it was a promise I'd never kept.

Now, sitting on my bed, reflecting my thoughts turned back again. Only this time my thoughts turned all the way back, back to the day he first confided in me.

It was a warm day in the early spring of 1943 and the fields of Tennessee were playing host to the U.S. 5th Armored Division. We were on Tennessee maneuvers and we were between "battles." It was Sunday, a day of rest, and men and tanks were sprawled out every which way without regard to any strict confining military formation.

Our tank, the platoon lead tank, was reposed in an isolated spot in the shade of some trees some fifty yards away from the rest of our platoon. No one was about and I was sitting on the ground, my back resting against a tree alongside our tank, writing letters. I was enjoying the eloquence of my writing when my thoughts were interrupted by a voice that called out from the inside of our tank. "Hey, Vic," the voice said, "when you're through with your letter, if you'll write one to my mother for me I'll clean the turret and sponsons for you."

Now I'd known my tank driver for about a year and like most people he liked to kid around a bit, so I ignored the voice from the tank and continued writing my letter. I had just finished sealing the envelope and had started to walk in the direction of the mail clerk's tent, but Bill, who was now out of the tank, was standing in front of me, blocking my way.

"Maybe you didn't hear me," he said, "but I just said I'd clean the turret and sponsons for you if you'd write my mother for me."

He looked sincere as he spoke, but I still felt he had to be kidding, so I just looked at him and said, "Knock it off, Bill. Writing's not that much of a chore to you. Forget the tank, write your mom yourself."

Well, he just stood there looking at me steadily, and then without batting an eye, he said, "If I could write I wouldn't ask you."

That shook me up. What he said and the way he said it rang true, but it didn't add up.

Bill Aldy was a rugged, good-natured fellow from the backwoods of Mississippi, and on the surface, at least, he was well-adjusted in the Army. An excellent tank driver, well-oriented in the field, and good with weapons; he was a good soldier in any man's Army. Along with these qualifications, he was quite personable and intelligent.

To my mind, at least, these things didn't allow for illiteracy, but, then, I wasn't too informed about illiteracy. At any rate, this wasn't the time for reflection. Not with his words, "If I could write I wouldn't ask you," hanging in the air.

"I can write my name," Bill offered, "but that's about the size of it."

With that I said simply, "Sorry I misunderstood, Bill. I'll be glad to write your mother for you." So I wrote the letter, naturally in his vernacular. After it was completed I read it back to him. That was the start of it. Soon I was writing not only his mother, but all of his relatives and friends.

At the outset it occurred to me that perhaps I could teach him to read and write, so I tried teaching him the alphabet and sound of each letter. Bill caught on to the rudiments of spelling and was able to form a number of single syllable words. But his progress was slow and painful for him. When I perceived that he was becoming disgusted and depressed with his progress, I abandoned the idea of trying to teach him. Instead, I tried to convince him that we should look into going to an Army school. But Bill had had enough of schooling ideas when he was a child in Mississippi and there was no way he'd even consider giving it a shot. All he wanted was someone who would read and write letters for him and be quiet about it. So I became his "write hand man."

Because I handled all of Bill's correspondence, I had more knowledge of him and his background than probably anyone else in our outfit. And with that knowledge came understanding.

It was from his mother that I was allowed to get a glimpse of what made Bill the strong, rugged, yet gentle man he was. Her letters were simple, yet touching. "Take care, Bill, I'm so glad to know you have so many friends." "Don't forget to thank your kind friend who writes for you"..... and always the ending "Trust in Christ and God."

It was easy to learn the rest from Bill. I don't remember what occasioned it, but I remember Bill once told me how it came about that he successfully avoided school.

"We're the only state in the uh (you'll excuse the expression) 'the Union', where a kid doesn't have to go to school."

"No compulsory educational laws?"

"That's right. Pop knew the few brushes I'd had with school and book learning and he knew it just wasn't for me. Pop's a good guy, and Mom, well, she just went along with it." It was a pretending game and Bill told it like this:

They were in the kitchen, the three of them. Bill's Mom and Dad and little Bill, aged six or seven. The breakfast plates were in the sink and the menfolk were getting ready for the day. "We're a goin' to school, Momma, and we'll be awalking'. Just Dad and me." And Dad would smile and press his small son's hand in his, and then both of them would kiss Momma good-bye and they'd be off. Only it wasn't to school they'd be a goin', they were a goin' fishin'."

Bill's home, Sallis, was a field of God's nestled somewhere in the lush greenery of Mississippi. All around Sallis lay spacious low sloping hills and fields, and interspersed in those sloping hills and fields were trees, lots of trees and forests through which ran streams and rivers. And sometimes hunting among the trees and fishing in the rivers and streams were little Bill and his father. These were scenes I could see vividly as Bill would describe them to me.

Of course there was a lot more to Bill's life than just hunting and fishing. There was work. Although he didn't care for schoolwork which called for book larnin', Bill was industrious, and being industrious he found his rewards in learning manual skills. By the time he had reached his early teens he could operate a tractor and run the machinery needed to manage a farm. (From driving tractors to driving tanks, so Bill said, was really a very simple changeover.)

Because we lived in a structural and mechanical environment and because he could do almost anything where mechanical skills were called for, Bill was a literate man in our world; in a sense more literate than many people who could read and write (including me).

Yet, despite his competence in our world, I was aware that somewhere deep inside Bill felt a gnawing sense of frustration over his illiteracy. Once or twice, when Bill had had a little too much to drink, his feelings of inadequacy surfaced and he made a couple of self-deprecating remarks about himself. It was nothing to be concerned about because for the most part, Bill had a positive and optimistic personality, and he had a good sense of self-esteem, but the remarks did indicate that he felt keenly over his shortcoming.

When I first started writing for Bill, he told me that all of his friends and relatives knew of his illiteracy. That is, all except one. And that one exception was his girlfriend.

"Mississippi Gal" wrote nice, sweet, homespun type letters to Bill. From what she wrote, it appeared that she held a special place in her heart for him. Although nothing of s serious note was ever gone into, judging from what Bill asked me to write, she was very definitely his girl.

I enjoyed writing to "Mississippi Gal" because I didn't have to be too careful in writing exactly what Bill said. I remember one night when Bill wanted a letter written to her, his total input was "Tell her I miss her apple pies, and the walking in the moonlight stuff." After these brief instructions, Bill took off for the PX.

So I took it from there and wrote his girl a light-hearted letter saying that he was longing desperately for her, longing for the night he'd go for a stroll in the moonlight with her, clutching one of her apple pies.

When I'd read these lines to Bill later, telling him what "we'd" written, he responded with a big laugh, and referring to himself, said, "Man! I never knew I could write so good!"

Some of Bill's home-grown expressions were lazily drawled; however, when he wished to emphasize a point strongly he usually relied on the word "guarantee," and he used it in split form, saying, "I guaran-cotton-pickin' – tee ya!" (only he didn't say cotton pickin'). At times, when I heard this I would remind Bill that splitting words like this was not acceptable in higher social levels and I would further caution him that such misuse of the English language could lead him into the heinous crime of splitting an infinitive. To this latter charge Bill spoke reassuringly to me, saying, "I don't split none of them things, and I don't associate with the low-life who do." And for emphasis, he would add, "I guaran....' tee ya that!"

I liked the way he spoke English, but I liked his sense of loyalty and friendship even more.

Many months before I had started to write Bill's letters, I had on occasion run into him at a sociable crap game in the company area. Although these times were infrequent, I noticed that Bill always bet with me, never against me. And the reason for that was his sense of loyalty to me as a true friend prevented him from wanting to win money from me.

Knowing his high regard for the truth, I had sometimes wondered if in the back of his mind he might have felt concern over the day he would return home after the war had ended, and he'd tell his girl he didn't personally write his letters.

Now, on learning of his death, I realized all the plans he had made for the day when he would return to his girl and his beloved home in Mississippi had vanished into thin air. All that remained of Bill Aldy was a memory. A memory of a strong and friendly comrade, who never intended harm to anyone. A man whose loyal and benign spirit was redeemed by God during a battle in World War II.

LA KOOK DOOR OPENS

The pass was high. I reached up, snared it, faked a two-handed set shot, dribbled, whirled right around the one man that stood between me and the basket, and went in for a perfect lay-up at the door. In retracing my steps back down the court I again passed "Doc," the man I'd faked out and dribbled by so easily. "Doc" was standing in the middle of the aisle, between rows of beds.

"Did you score?" Doc asked.

"You know very well I did," I beamed, kicking the imaginary basketball away. "But you should've been able to stop me, Doc. How many times have I stressed defense to you?" (He was always poor defensively.)

The doctor veered off. "I spoke to your brother in my office for ten seconds last weekend and I asked him to give you a message. Could you tell me if he relayed the message to you, and if so, what it was?" Doctor Sherry looked straight into my eyes, not cracking a smile.

I sobered a bit. "Yes, sir. My brother told me that you said I should stop pulling your leg."

"That's very good," the doctor replied. "I see your memory is in good shape."

The serious expression on Doc's face had eased somewhat and something like amusement showed in his eyes. "Corporal Norber," he said, repressing a smile, "How would you like to play golf tomorrow with real golf balls?"

"This is it! This is it!" I thought. It was common knowledge that Fitz had a real neat nine hole golf course, and Doc knew from my record that golf was my favorite sport.

"You mean it? You're not kidding? You're not pulling *my* leg? I'm going to the open ward?"

"Tomorrow morning."

VAN ARKEL

His face was drawn, firm, and rocklike. It spoke of great strength; it had the appearance of having been hewn from granite. He was close to six feet and the rest of him had been granite-like too. He had a massive chest in which there was a massive hole. The hole, created by shrapnel, was so large it looked like I could put my entire fist into it. Still conscious, he was bleeding and in agony, as two medics were helping him reach the rubble that had been the first floor of a small farmhouse. At the top of the stairs that led into the basement his knees sagged. I was standing by to see if I could be of any assistance. The badly wounded man looked at the medics and me. "Get out of here," he mumbled, "save yourselves. Leave, leave me, forget me, forget me." He wanted to be left behind, left alone to die. He'd done everything right, everything a thinking, competent courageous tank commander could possibly do right, he did. Now he was dying. He'd do that right, too.

His concern was not for himself. Despite his gaping wound he was still in command of his senses. And as consciousness was leaving him, his last thought was of his comrades.

I was standing on the first tee at Fitzsimons, gazing down the fairway. Yesterday had been my first day out of "locked" and I'd spent the entire day on the golf course. I was reflecting on my play of yesterday; I'd split the fairway with a good shot, hit the approach well, two-putted from twenty feet, and got my par. Not bad, after a four year layoff. I was hoping I'd do as well today. In the fresh open air of the Rockies, I was starting to live again.

"Hey, Norber," someone called from a short distance behind me.

I turned and looked behind me, toward the street. A patient in reds, on a bicycle in the street some fifty feet away, was pointing at me, waving for me to come over. When he repeated my name I started walking over to see what he wanted. I must've gotten about half-way when suddenly I recognized him. "Good God! Van Arkel! I can't believe it!" I shouted. "You're alive, you're alive!"

"Well, of course I'm alive, Norber," he said. "What the hell do you think? I'm dead? Do you see any dead people around here? Everybody around here is alive!"

The excitement of the moment was too much for me. I'd last seen Van in Bergstein, at the top of the basement steps. "When I last saw you, you had a great big hole in your chest and you were losing consciousness fast!"

"So," he said calmly, "I came around on Christmas." (He was wounded on December 6).

He didn't allow any further remarks about himself, as he quickly asked, "What are you doing out here?"

"They say I'm nuts," I told him.

In reply he laughed, "So, tell me something new!"

Seeing Van alive, realizing he was really real and all in one piece, listening to him joking and wisecracking was having a more wholesome effect on me than any other I'd experienced since Hurtgen. I could've talked with him for the rest of the morning. I wanted to, but when I suggested we talk things over at the PX, he said it would have to wait until the afternoon because the doctors wanted him out bike-riding for reasons of health. Before pedaling away he told me where he was located in the hospital and asked me to drop by in the afternoon after I'd played golf.

When I got to his room that afternoon, I found him with his jacket off, exercising with an apparatus that was over his bed. His entire chest had an overlapping fold of flesh, flesh that had been grafted from his legs. Obviously he had undergone an extreme amount of surgery. From what he told me and what I could see, all had gone well for him, but he still had quite a distance to go yet.

For the most part, we didn't dwell on the present, but rather on the past and the things we had in common, our company and battalion. A sad note crept into our conversation once or twice, but most of the memories we spoke of were of good times and good things that had happened to us.

When supper time rolled around and it was time for me to leave, Van asked me to visit with him again soon, when I had some free time like after I'd finished playing golf.

I'd been straightforward with Van. I'd minced no words in telling him I'd had battle fatigue. Though battle fatigue was considered a stigma during those days, Van accepted me, battle fatigue and all my other neuroses. He was a real friend, and when he asked me to visit him again, I assured him I would. Definitely.

THE LAYOUT THE WAY OUT AND OUT

The thing I liked about golf was it got me out into the wide open spaces, gave me a sense of freedom or at least half-way freedom; for that's what I was, half free. The game or the score didn't matter too much; I had better things to think about. And I thought about them a good deal as I would walk down the fairways humming and whistling my favorite song, "Don't Fence Me In" (from George Gershwin's "Girl Crazy"). Another good thing about the freedom of these grounds was my thoughts were my own and no government psychiatrist could violate the privacy of my thoughts.

Not being fenced in was one part of golf I enjoyed, but one of the benefits I liked most were the fantasies I could indulge in while walking. My favorite fantasy started as soon as I left the first tee, and it was induced by the layout of the course itself; for along the left side of the first fairway ran a tall, weedy, narrow rough, and running parallel to that, and the only thing that kept the rough in the hospital grounds, was a long chain link fence. Just looking down that fence-line would bring on the vision: *"I'd hook that first shot wildly, high and far over that fence. And after that I'd walk down the fairway a couple of hundred yards and then I'd saunter through the tall weeds of the narrow rough and climb over the fence. And then, standing out there on the street where my golf ball should be, would be this beautiful, blue-eyed blonde, all curvy and slim and trim and wearing a sheer, very sheer, white blouse, and she'd be holding my golf ball in her hand and she'd look at me with her sexy bedroom eyes, and she'd have her car nearby.*" For variations on my fantasies I'd sometimes make the girl a brunette with brown eyes, or maybe she'd have auburn hair with green eyes.

Despite my imaginative masterpieces, my golf game didn't suffer. I was to all outward appearances a decent golfer with a decent mind. My golfing companions seemed to enjoy my company and I believed I was gaining a favorable impression on my doctor who I knew was receiving periodic reports about my behavior on the golf links.

So it came as a great shock to me when Doc Sherry came to my ward one evening to tell me he was considering putting me on insulin therapy.

Being in an open ward, I naturally assumed all such drug treatments were behind me. Having had a bad trip from intravenous insulin treatments, I reacted badly to the suggestion that I again receive insulin. I told the doctor he could forget insulin, I'd had a ton of it shoved into my veins before.

He replied the treatments he wanted me to have were intramuscular, not intravenous, and the dosage would be much less.

We argued a bit and I demanded to know how many more treatments I would be forced to undergo and how much longer they planned to keep me before they set me free. That ended the insulin threat.

August rolled around and I knew it was August and that was good. I sought out Dr. Sherry late one afternoon after playing golf all day, and explained to him that I was very anxious to leave the hospital. "School will be opening soon and I want to return to civilian life as soon as possible so I can make plans for furthering my education."

"That's a good reason," Doc Sherry agreed. "But school is almost two months away. What's your big hurry? Why are you so anxious to get out of this hospital right now? I'd like to know what's so urgent for you that you want to leave immediately. Think about this: here, at this hospital, you can play golf five days a week, eat fried chicken for supper, drink Cokes at the PX any time you want. What in heaven's name is so terrible about this hospital?

"Nothing's terrible about this hospital," I countered. "It's just that there's a lot more to life than golf and fried chicken."

"And don't forget the Cokes," he reminded me.

As I stood looking at this kindly doctor, I was wondering if I'd ever get a girl in my arms again, wondering if my doctor needed a refresher course in Freud.

A few days later, Doc Sherry met me at the entrance to the ward. It seemed a chance meeting, but the words he spoke sounded very official. "Arrangements are being made for you to be discharged. Tomorrow morning you are to go to the Administration Building where you will sign some papers that have to be signed in order that your discharge papers may be processed. Stay on the ward tomorrow morning until I give you instructions as to the room you're to report to and the exact time you're to report. Any questions?"

Elated at the good news, I had no questions. On being dismissed, I ran over to Van's ward to tell him of my good luck. I expected Van to share in my happiness, but I found him skeptical. "You say your doctor is a psychiatrist and he thinks you're sane? Hmmmm!"

On the morning of the following day I was at my bed waiting for Doc Sherry to drop by with my instructions as to where and when to report at the Administrations Building. The papers I was to sign, as I understood, or assumed from briefly talking with the doctor, were mere forms that had to be signed so that I could get my discharge papers processed. I thought they would be papers relating to my financial status or some other such trivial matter. But it turned out to be a matter of much greater importance.

At first I couldn't believe what I was hearing. The attendant who was giving me my instructions (Doc Sherry sent my instructions via messenger) was informing me that the papers I was to sign were medical disability claims against the government. On hearing this, I became very upset with the attendant and started arguing that I would sign no claim against the government of the United States. I insisted I was to get an honorable discharge, not a medical discharge.

The poor attendant, whom the doctor had sent to give me this horrendous news, did his best to explain to me that the medical discharge I was to receive was also an honorable one. But his argument didn't sit well with me, so instead of wasting words and time with him I took off to find Doc Sherry.

I didn't see him in his office, but I found him hiding on the sidewalk in front of my ward. As soon as I saw him, I let fly with my thoughts. I let him know in no uncertain terms that I was nuts when I first volunteered for service and I would sign no disability claims against the government.

For some reason completely beyond me, his only response was, "When you sign the claim your discharge papers can be processed." Then he refused to talk any further to me and he turned and went on his way. That was the start of my last disagreement with Doc Sherry.

Every day for about a week I'd bug this good doctor, "You got my discharge papers ready yet?"

And every day his answer was always the same. "Have you been to the Administration Building and signed your claim papers yet?" He could really be annoying.

Anyway, after about a week of trying to make sense with him and trying to impress on him the need to keep our national budget down, I felt myself weakening. Besides, my fantasies on the golf course were getting worse, so one day shortly after the A Bomb explosions and shortly after the cease-fire order of August 15, 1945, I laid down my golf sticks and walked to the Administration Building to sign my surrender. I felt like Lee at Appomattox.

On the morning of August 24, 1945, after saying goodbye to Van Arkel, I paused briefly at the gates of Fitzsimons General Hospital, Denver, Colorado. I paused so I could have one last look at the hospital, and the Army. No bugles blared, no trumpets. I'd been given an honorable discharge and released in my own custody. Aside from my discharge, the only other item I valued was the autographed booklet, which

I valued, lay carefully placed in my duffel bag.

HOME

It was a great feeling to wake up in the morning and realize no one was looking over my shoulder, observing me, making notes about my behavior or speech. I was home. I was free.

Our apartment faced the street and was on the second floor of a three story, twelve family apartment building which was located in a quiet sector of the west end of St. Louis. Our home was fully furnished, the furniture having been purchased from the previous tenants who had moved out and sublet the apartment to my family. My sister had made all the arrangements, with Dad's financial backing, and set up the home she had envisioned when she had visited me at Fitzsimons.

We were a family again, closely knit, living under one roof. There were at this time three of us: my father, my sister and I. But my brother would be joining us in the near future after his separation from service.

My home situation was precisely what Doc Sherry had had in mind when he had explained to me the reason I was being given an "early discharge" from Fitzsimons. "We are releasing you at this time," he had said, "because we feel you can convalesce better at home than you can in the hospital."

And convalesce I would.

My first few days at home saw me looking up a few close relatives and friends and spending a little time with them. My evenings were spent quietly in the company of my sister, dining out with her after she came home from work, and afterwards returning to the apartment, where we both would sit and talk and listen to the radio. Of course, prior to my coming home, I had anticipated going out and painting the town red, but at that time I had not foreseen that I would be tense and anxious when out among people.

Unaccountably, I was jittery for a while. Fortunately, though, my jitters disappeared as quickly as they had come.

After spending a week or so around the apartment, I began to feel the warm juices of life surging through my veins, urging me to go forth in pursuit of life, love and happiness. Or, simply put, I wanted a girl in my arms.

Taking heed of the popular notion that the quickest way to get a nice girl in my arms was to ask her to dance with me, I headed for the nearest dance hall. And it was there, my long-deserved vacation, which would last all of two or three weeks, began.

Dancing to the sounds of big band music in the city's more popular ballrooms, occasionally meeting a girl there and going out on a date afterwards, was sheer heaven to me. I was back in the swing of life again and enjoying every minute of it.

As the end of September neared and my vacation drew to a close, I felt well-rested and confident and ready to meet what I knew would be a real challenge to me – school!

To get a college education had been a dream of mine since I had graduated high school. At that time, because of so many unfavorable circumstances, the dream seemed unattainable. Now, it appeared my dream would come true.

On enrolling in Washington University I designated journalism as my major, knowing at the time that this fine institution was lacking a school of journalism. For help in choosing my subjects I was referred to the Dean of Men. On hearing I had chosen journalism for my major, the Dean asked why I didn't enroll at Missouri University, an institution known for its outstanding school of journalism.

In reply I said that in readjusting to civilization and civilian life, I wanted to live at home as long as possible while attending school. And since I could earn at Washington University the credits required for entrance into any school of journalism, I saw no reason in going elsewhere to earn my pre-journalism credits.

This explanation satisfied the Dean, so he then turned his attention to scheduling courses that would enable me to transfer to Missouri University in two years. My subjects, incidentally, included the usual 101 liberal arts courses of History, Political Science, English, Spanish and Geology.

At the outset everything seemed to go smoothly. In English I had written one assignment and was promptly promoted to an advanced English class. I was also doing well in three of my other studies. My poor subject was geology, but I hoped to be able to get a grip on it before it threw me. Sometimes given a little time, things work out, sometimes they don't.

Halfway through October I began to fear the worst. I was unable to comprehend geology to any degree and I knew that I would fail the subject. Failing to comprehend anything can be very frustrating to a normal person, but to one beset with emotional problems of guilt and an extreme lack of self-confidence, frustration could produce anxieties I could not handle.

Suddenly, without any warning, I began to experience seizure-like attacks during the night. Again, I would be abruptly awakened from my sleep by feelings of paralysis over my entire body. All of my muscles cramped and my jaws were clamped tightly, preventing me from crying out for help. These were the same types of attacks I had known previously while sleeping in combat zones.

By the end of October the handwriting was on the wall. I was failing geology and in some of my other classes I was starting to slip. The final straw occurred around the last day of the month. The attack had started as usual with a cramping in my muscles. Following that I experienced an out-of-body sensation in which I felt warm and undulating waves pass over me and then I heard a soft female voice. After that, nothing.

On awakening in the morning I felt tired, very tired. I remembered the voice and I felt it would be wise for me to withdraw from school.

Before going to the registrar's office to withdraw, I felt I should speak personally to my English teacher, a sweet, white-haired elderly lady who had been a source of encouragement to me and was responsible for my being an A student in her class.

She was seated at her desk; class had not yet started, when I broke the news to her.

On hearing that I was leaving she asked to speak privately with me in the hallway.

She spoke to me not only as a teacher, but as a friend. She said I showed great promise as a writer and she pleaded with me to reconsider my decision, saying if I quit school I'd be throwing away my life.

In reply I said that I really was not college material. I did not mention my geological fault, but I did say my shortcoming in science was enough to convince me I wasn't really cut out for college.

She sensed that I was distressed over my failure, but she refused to accept me as being "unscientific." Instead, she repeated herself saying if I quit now, I was throwing my life away.

In her hands she held my last in-class writing assignment, which had not yet been returned to me. At the top of the first page appeared my grade, A-, and below that the reason for the minus – forty two errors in grammar and punctuation.

"Does this look like you're not college material?" she asked.

She tried, she tried very hard to dissuade me, but in the end I knew that I must do what I must do. At a convenient pause in the discussion, I excused myself saying I really had to be getting on my way. And with that, I walked down the long hall to the exit.

As I neared the exit door, I heard behind me the clip-clop of her shoes. She was pursuing me. She just wouldn't give up.

I turned from the door and returned to her, meeting her halfway in the hall. She had thought of a solution for my problems. "Go home," she said, "go home for a week and just rest, don't make any decisions now, you're too upset; promise me that you'll just go home and rest for one week."

I couldn't promise her that, I said, but I could promise her I'd always remember her.

As we went our separate ways, I do believe she was as sad at my leaving school as I was.

My first year at home saw many changes take place. Shortly after my brother returned from the Army, my sister got married and left, and shortly after her leaving, my brother too, got married and moved out. When my brother moved out, Dad informed me that my cousin, Jerry, with whom I'd enlisted in the Army in 1942, had expressed an interest in joining us in the apartment. Dad, incidentally, had lived with Jerry's family after Mom's death, and had lived with them until the time he reestablished our present household; so the relationship with my cousin and his family was quite special. I was, of course, keen on the idea of Jerry coming to live with us, so Dad invited him over.

I had had many problems following my release from service. Simply put, I was removed from the psycho ward, but the psycho ward was not removed from me. Whereas my self-esteem was low before I entered college, now, following that scholastic debacle, my self-esteem was nonexistent. In no time I found myself in a blue funk. There were, however, a number of saving graces on my side – I had my own family, lived at home, and was financially secure and independent. I was financially well-off because at the time of my discharge, in addition to my mustering out pay, I also received some back pay due me. And added to this "monetary stockpile" were numerous war bonds I had purchased throughout the war. So I had no financial worries, but I was depressed.

When my cousin came to live with us he didn't approve of my sitting around the house. He said I'd wear out the furniture; I was home too much and he wasn't going to tolerate it!

Although he knew nothing of my personal finances, he took it upon himself to see to it that I should receive everything I was entitled to receive from the government. I was unaware that at some time around the conclusion of the war, the government had set up an unemployment bureau for returning veterans which enabled unemployed veterans to collect twenty dollars a week for fifty-two weeks. Veterans who received such unemployment compensation were referred to as being members of the 52-20 club.

When cousin Jerry arrived on the family scene and heard I knew nothing of the 52-20 club, he berated me for being ignorant and stupid. In reply to these charges I admitted I was a mystery even unto myself. I never seemed to know that the government was passing bills aimed at helping people like me. I recalled that I first heard of the educational benefits which were granted me from brother, Ted. That I was too stupid to be able to take advantage of those benefits was another matter, but my ignorance of government benefits was truly appalling.

At any rate, despite my ignorance and stupidity, I hastened to the unemployment office where I became a charter member of the 52-20 club.

With funds being no problem, I withdrew from the labor market until sometime in 1946, at which time I started looking for a job. At first I took any job offered me. Once I was a shoe salesman, then an office clerk, and once I worked mornings in a tobacco shop which totally unbeknownst to me was the locale of a big gambling group known as "The Town Game."

This last fact became known to me one morning as I sat eating my breakfast and reading the morning newspaper. "Town Game Raided!" screamed the headlines. And below the headlines I saw pictures of my boss getting into a police paddy wagon. At that I turned to the want-ads.

Anyhow, by 1949 I had been living an aimless life drifting from one job to another, not caring and not worrying about anything. The fact that I was getting nowhere fast didn't seem to phase me. I had no great responsibilities, no family to support, so I gave no thought to the future.

My father, however, was very much concerned about my work habits and my future. He couldn't understand how I could hop from one meaningless clerical job to another.

Twice in three years he'd attempted to take me into his real estate business with him, and on each occasion I begged out. After my second and last unsuccessful attempt to become a businessman, I returned to the clerical field where I felt more comfortable. I was able to support myself and live decently well.

But Pop was worried.

ABRAHAM SKUY

The years following the conclusion of the war passed swiftly. For me it was a time of peace and tranquility, a time of forgetfulness: I had forgotten the war and what had happened to me and my old outfit, the 5th Armored Division. Despite my shiftless lifestyle, I was happy.

One cold night in January of 1949, while I was relaxing comfortably in the living room reading a book, I heard a fumbling at the front doorknob and a key being inserted in the door lock. Although it was around midnight or later and I was alone, I was not alarmed because I knew who was at the door. It was my father returning home from his night work at his usual late hour.

When the door opened, I glanced up and noticed that he was accompanied by a stranger. Both men looked tired, probably from a strenuous evening of crap-shooting, I thought, as I knew Dad had gone across the river earlier that evening with that in mind. My thought was confirmed when Dad introduced the stranger to me as Abe Sky.

"Sky's the limit," said the stranger, extending his hand, "only it's spelled S-K-U-Y."

"Glad to meet you, Mr. Skuy," I responded. "Isn't that an unusual way to spell sky?"

"It's South African."

"Oh, you're from South Africa," I said, noting his unusual dialect.

"Well, yes, I was originally," he replied, "but now I'm from Van Buren, Arkansas, and I'm here in St. Louis on a business trip.

I studied Mr. Skuy momentarily.

He looked to be of Dutch descent, with light blue eyes, a short straight nose and a full head of graying hair. Although well-dressed in a Hickey Freeman pin stripe, he didn't appear to be the executive type. While he spoke, a cigarette draped from the corner of his mouth and hung dryly and precariously from the edges of his lips. He didn't use the ashtray at his elbow, but rather let the ashes that accumulated on the cigarette fall carelessly on the lapels of his otherwise spotless suit coat.

Recalling that native South Africans of Dutch descent were called Boers, I asked, "Are you a Boer, Mr. Skuy?"

Mr. Skuy shot me a pained look like he'd been insulted. Then he responded, "Well, if I'm a bore I'll guarantee you you'll find me an interesting bore!"

We both smiled at this and then as our ensuing conversation began to unfold it became obvious that the stranger had been modest in describing himself as "interesting."

We were discussing his background, life in South Africa, and Mr. Skuy was telling Dad and me of his days as a wrestler back in the wrestling clubs of Johannesburg, and he told his story so vividly it seemed that we could smell the cigar smoke at ringside. Skuy didn't dwell on his brief career as a wrestler. But quickly and smoothly from ringside, Dad and I were mentally transported dockside to the harbor of Capetown, South Africa, where Skuy was standing on the deck of an ocean liner that was leaving for New York. Standing there dockside with Dad and me waving goodbye to Skuy were his dearest friends, most of whom were poker players, crap shooters, with a few bad pony players thrown in. And as the boat was pulling out of the harbor, we could hear his friends shouting to him, "Steer clear of those gambling houses in the U.S. of A." This Dad and I could hear through the flapping of seagull's wings and the ship's fog horn.

"Now you see why everyone says Skuy's the limit," Dad whispered to me as Skuy paused to catch his breath before continuing.

"Now it was not too long after World War I and I was living in New York City when I happened to run across a salvage operation that was taking place outside New York harbor. The operation was in deep financial water; it needed $100,000 to keep it going so it could come to a successful conclusion. Now I went out and looked at this operation first-hand and I saw that this could be my chance of a lifetime to make a fortune. But $100,000 wasn't exactly a piece of change I carried around on me. So for that kind of money I went to a good friend of mine, Harry Sinclair, the oil magnate, whom I had happened to meet one night in a gambling establishment, and I told him about the operation and offered him in on the deal, saying we'd share in the profits equally. I even proposed a deal where we'd each be in for fifty grand a piece, that way I only needed fifty thousand. but Harry was a sporty guy, not greedy, and he says to me that the oil on land has him plenty occupied. So he just said he'd lend me the $100,000. So he gave me the hundred grand and I gave him my marker. No business deal, no promissory notes. Just my marker.

"Anyhow, as it turned out, this salvage operation is a big success, and I wind up with profits coming out of my ears. Unfortunately, though, the week the payoff comes, the ponies are running at Narragansett."

Skuy's face took on a downcast look. "So, there I was, standing in Harry Sinclair's office explaining what went wrong at the track, and I was telling him I felt so bad about losing all the money that I feel like shooting myself."

"And Harry, on hearing this, suddenly opens his desk drawer. I swear I thought he was going to help me to my earthly end. But no, when he withdraws his hand from the drawer he waves before me my marker for $100,000, which he promptly tears up. "You'll make it good, Abe," was all he said. But then he said more. I have your word, and I know you. I don't need any markers."

And Skuy concluded this story, saying, "Of course, later on when I made a bundle in oil, I repaid Harry the entire amount."

By the time Skuy finished this story the hour was quite late, and we all felt it was time to retire. Dad and I retired to our beds, and Skuy slept on a bed we made for him on the sofa.

Early the next morning when I arose, I found Skuy gone. He had gotten up bright and early and was on his way back to his home in Van Buren, Arkansas.

For the next couple of months Skuy visited our house several times. It appeared to me that he and Dad were planning some sort of business deal together, but I had no idea what sort of deal they had in mind, until one day in March when my father surprised me with:

"Abe has secured a location for our store on the main street in Fort Smith, Arkansas."

"What store?" I asked.

"It's a combination Army and civilian goods store we're opening in Fort Smith. You and Abe are going to run the store and I'm going to supply the financial backing."

Abe and Dad had worked out this whole deal without once telling me of their plans, even though I was included in them. Several factors were suddenly revealed to me that were supposed to persuade me to be amenable to the deal.

First, Fort Smith was an Army town and the economy of the town boomed because of the Army payroll. And second, the unit stationed at the nearby Army camp was the 5th Armored Division. Not only would I learn how to make money and become a successful businessman, but I'd enjoy seeing my old outfit again. So Abe had explained the set-up to Dad.

On hearing this I immediately rebelled. I told my father that I preferred living in St. Louis and that the outfit stationed at Camp Chaffee, located outside Fort Smith, was not my old outfit, but was probably a training unit I didn't care about. I really felt I should have been consulted. Dad's response to my objections was brief. He'd sunk a bundle in this, and it had all been done with my future in mind. The idea of my old outfit stationed nearby while I learned how to become a businessman under the tutelage of our friend Abe Skuy appealed to my father.

In view of everything riding on this venture, I consented to go to Fort Smith. But I knew I wouldn't like it!

I liked it, I liked it. The store opened the first week in April of 1949, and it was flooded with GI's wearing the familiar 5th Armored Division patch. Seeing the emblem brought back very strong memories, but they were not sad memories nor was there a sense of guilt. Oddly enough, I enjoyed talking with anyone connected with the 5th because we had a lot in common, even though this outfit was not the men I had served with.

Our store prospered during the spring and most of the summer of '49. The camp was filled to capacity, and business was good everywhere in Fort Smith. As a matter of fact, things were too good.

The bad news came out late that summer. A directive from Washington, D.C., ordering the closing of a number of military camps across the country. Camp Chaffee was among them.

By November the camp was emptied except for a skeleton crew. Since most of our customers were GI's, the camp's closing meant curtains for our store.

Dad lost a bundle in the business venture, but he accepted his loss philosophically: Life's a game, you win some, you lose some, so this time we lost."

A little over two years elapsed following the store's closing before Skuy reappeared out of the blue. It was spring, 1952, and my former business associate paid me an unexpected visit in St. Louis. On learning that I was free to travel, he asked if I'd care to accompany him on a stock buying trip to Dallas, Texas. As I always enjoyed the pleasure of his company, I readily accepted.

The trip was routed through Fort Smith, because Skuy had to finalize plans with his business partners who were located there. After spending one day there finalizing and loading up on money, we were on our way.

As we crossed the Arkansas State Line, Oklahoma and Springtime seemed to merge and come into view at the same time. Everywhere the beautiful fields were freshly arrayed in green; shrubs and trees were blossoming, and birds were chirping. All was right with Mother Nature, but not with Skuy!

He had his incurable disease – Gambling! Although he could make money easily, his gambling habits kept him forever broke, hurting not only himself, but his lovely wife and daughter as well. He needed help to overcome this affliction and as a former crap-shooter, one who had completely overcome the addiction of gambling, I knew I could be of immense aid to Abe, so I started talking.

First, I very tactfully stressed to him the good aspects of his character, his devotion to his family, his industriousness, and his sense of humor. Abe was interested and a good listener. Then I eased into the subject of gambling and what it had done to his life. In a few minutes Abe saw the problem clearly; he agreed there was a strong need for change and reformation. As a matter of fact, so strongly did he agree that despite the fact that we were traveling 80 miles an hour, he started pounding the steering wheel with his left hand and jamming his right into the roof of the car swearing on the lives of his loved ones, wife, daughter, and dog, in that order, that'd he'd never gamble again so long as he lived. And as I watched the Oklahoma landscape fly by, I felt it wouldn't be too difficult an oath to keep. Anyhow, when he finished swearing I knew he was a changed man. The beads of perspiration that stood out on his forehead testified he had seen the light!

We must've driven about fifteen minutes in silence following his reformation, when suddenly we swerved off the highway onto the gravel lot of a filling station. Abruptly, he turned to me saying, "I'd better phone ahead to those people in Dallas, to assure them I'm on my way and will consummate the business deal tomorrow. We're running a little late and I don't want them to have any doubts about me." With that, he hurried into the station to make his phone call.

While he was gone, I stretched out for a little nap. I must have been more tired than I realized, for when I awoke and looked at my watch I noticed I had dozed almost an hour. Still no sign of Abe. Suddenly I remembered the big bank roll he was carrying and became alarmed. So, I got out of the car and went into the filling station to look for him.

On entering the station I noticed that there was a stairway leading to a room above the station. And from this room I could hear muffled voices. I raced up the stairs but I was too late; the look of despair on Abe's face told the story. The dice on the gambling table told the rest.

It was a long journey back to Fort Smith. Abe tried to convince me he had called Dallas and learned the deal was off, and just by some strange coincidence there happened to be a crap game going on in that filling station. Well, all I knew was, I hoped he could explain the situation to his partners with a more believable story.

Perhaps he did because shortly after our return to Fort Smith, he met with them. The meeting was brief and Abe emerged from it all smiles. "Vic," he said, "we're in great luck. Gotta new lead on a much better stock this time, but we gotta hurry to get this one. It's a real dandy and it's up for grabs. If we take turns driving and we drive all night, we should be able to make it by morning. How does Indianola, Mississippi sound to you?"

"Fine, Abe," I said, "think we'll make it?"

I had never before been to Mississippi or the Deep South, so I eagerly looked forward to this trip.

We started out late in the afternoon, drove all night and reached Indianola early the next morning. Without delay, we proceeded to Klumock's Department Store, the store Abe had come to see. While Abe entered into negotiations for the purchase of the stock, I stayed in the background as my presence was not needed. Seeing the large inventory in the store, there was no question that the negotiations would require several days before any settlement would be reached.

On about the third day, I was standing outside the store when the thought struck me, "I wonder where Sallis, Bill Aldy's home might be." I thought it improbable that anyone in the store would know, as it wasn't shown on the state maps which Abe and I had consulted while en route. Still, there was no harm in inquiring.

On entering the store, I saw two lady clerks standing a few feet apart from each other at a counter close by. I approached the one nearest to me and said, "Excuse me, could you tell me if you've ever heard of a place in Mississippi called Sallis?"

The clerk's eyes lit up in surprise, and she immediately turned to the other clerk, saying, "Miz Aldy, this man just asked me where Sallis is."

I was startled, caught completely off balance. "Is your name Aldy?" I blurted; "are you from Sallis?"

"Yes," she said, "that's right."

"Well," I stammered, "were you related to Bill Aldy, a tank driver in the Army during World War II?"

"Yes, we were kin." She appeared reluctant to discuss the matter. Perhaps she regarded me as a prying outsider. Whatever her reason, I decided not to pursue the family matter any further.

"Well, just how far is Sallis from here?" I asked.

"Oh, about 40 miles," Miz Aldy replied.

Out of the corner of my eye, I saw Skuy coming down the aisle to where we were standing.

"Well, Vic, are you ready to go out for some lunch?"

"Yeah, Abe, yeah," I nodded. I walked away with him completely mystified. "Abe," I asked, "you want to hear something unique?"

"What's on your mind, Vic?"

"Did you see that clerk, that lady I was talking to back in the store? Her name's Aldy," I exclaimed, "and she's from Sallis, Mississippi, and one of my best friends in the war was from Sallis, and his name was also Aldy, Bill Aldy; she was related to him."

"Well, that's quite a coincidence," Abe said, but before I had a chance to continue, Abe proceeded to tell me about an unusual experience of his own – another one of his many stories!

Abe, of course, didn't know the relationship that existed between Bill and me, and somehow, despite my excitement, I really didn't want to reveal confidential things that had been known only to Bill and me. So the matter was dropped, but not from my mind, for I was remembering Bill's words in jest: "Man, when you come down to Mississippi for a visit everywhere you look you're gonna' run into us Aldys." And now the first time I ever touched Mississippi soil, I ran right into an Aldy.

LOVE AT SECOND SIGHT

In the gathering dusk of a fall evening in 1953, I happened to be walking down a neighborhood sidewalk on my way to the corner drug store, where I planned to stop for a Coke and a sandwich. I was minding my own business, completely in control of myself, stable, and secure in the delusion that I was master of my fate. At this time I was single and could think like this. (Married people, I'd noticed, never appeared to me to be masters of their fate.)

As I approached the corner drug store, I noticed just ahead walking towards me, a young blond-haired girl of maybe nineteen or twenty. Someone new in the neighborhood, I thought, how pretty.

As this sweet creature was about to pass me, I chanced a glance in the direction of her face. It was only a brief glimpse I was afforded, but it was more than enough. For a moment I found myself bewitched, staring into the two loveliest green eyes ever I had seen. Her face was simply beautiful. Our eyes met in that moment and as she brushed by me, she smiled. It was a winsome smile. And I heard her say in a soft voice, "Hello, Vic."

I was taken aback, pushed off balance. How did this lovely girl know my name; where did she come from?

I turned about and let my eyes follow her. In the fading light of the evening I watched from a distance and saw her enter an apartment building. Very cautiously, yet quickly, I approached the building and watching from the sidewalk I caught a glimpse of her through a window as she rounded the second floor landing and headed for the third floor.

Suddenly the light snapped on in the front room of the third floor apartment facing the street. And in that instant it dawned on me that this beautiful stranger was not quite a stranger to me at all. As a matter of fact, I had met her only recently in a proper introduction, in this very same apartment into which I was now staring.

My thoughts came in a rush as I remembered the events that led up to our meeting:

A neighbor girl carrying a large bag of groceries was about to enter her apartment building when the bag suddenly broke and the groceries spilled to the ground. Being nearby, and being a gentleman, I immediately assisted her in gathering up the groceries and helping her deliver them to her apartment.

No sooner had we finished depositing the groceries on the dining room table, than I found myself being introduced to her roommate, a very strange looking girl.

"Vic, this is Jo." I stared wide-eyed at this strange looking creature. Two sparkling green eyes peered out at me from behind a pasty white face. Her face was all covered over with white goopy stuff and her hair was wrapped up in a towel, turban style. And the rest of her was wrapped in a chenille bathrobe. She looked like she was fresh from a shower.

"You'll please excuse my appearance," the green-eyed water sprite smiled. "It's Saturday night and I'm getting ready to go out on a date."

In response I said, "You're quite attractive." This I said kiddingly, for I had rarely been attracted to girls with white goopy stuff all over their face, but truth to say this girl did indeed have strikingly beautiful eyes. (So maybe I was only half-kidding.)

Now, as I stood outside her apartment in the gathering dusk recalling our meeting and how beautiful she looked as she passed me by in the street, all thoughts of a light bite at the drug store suddenly vanished from my mind and I turned and hurried back to my apartment and the telephone.

"Hello," cooed the sweet young voice on the other end of the line.

"Did you just say hello to me about two minutes ago?" I asked.

"If this is Vic, and I presume it is, then the answer is yes, I did."

After that brief opening, we made small talk. And as we talked I was seeing her in my mind's eyes. Her soft blonde hair falling loosely about the loveliest face ever created; her beautiful green eyes and sweet smile. And while we talked, one persistent question in the back of my mind kept bothering me: Would she go out with me?

When I finally verbalized the question and received an affirmative answer, I felt as elated as a teenager in love. I was young again, in my early thirties, but young.

And so we started going out together. And sometimes, while dining in a nightclub, staring across the table through a flickering candlelight into the endless beauty of two cool and limpid green eyes, I'd find myself thinking of marriage. Completely forgotten, blown from my mind, was the philosophy that married people are not masters of their fate. Such a thought never entered my mind these days; and even if it had, I doubt if I would have cared. I was smitten.

My courtship of Jo lasted two years and ended at the altar.

On New Year's Day of 1956, in a small setting in the living room of my beloved's home in the small town of Bristow, Oklahoma, we exchanged our wedding vows.

For seven years my honey and I knew marital bliss. Our home was blessed with three beautiful children. First a little girl, then a little boy, then another little girl.

We were a happy and loving family and very close. And then, suddenly, without warning, I was stricken with an illness that originated in an Army snake pit in England during World War II. And I had to leave my family to seek help at a V.A. Hospital.

WE MEET IN THE BLUE HAZE

I knew the date. It was January 8, 1963. I also knew my name, where I was, and how I got there.

I stood in the hallway peeking through a little window on the door of the doctor's office. The doctor had been shut up in his 9 by 12 cubicle for two solid hours, and being a notorious chain smoker, he had managed to hide himself somewhere in the middle of three packs of cigarette smoke and three chapters of his patient's case history – mine.

Suddenly the door swung open and I found myself facing the pall of smoke.

"Come in, Mr. Norber. Come in."

I entered the room slowly, and cautiously proceeded in the general direction of the voice.

"Well, what are you waiting for?" rasped the voice from somewhere in the room.

I hesitated in the pall a moment or so and then abruptly I saw the figure. He was seated at his desk halfway across the room, beyond the blue haze.

Dr. Gilpin was an intense, dedicated Veterans Administration medic who suffered from the delusion that he was a psychiatrist. Normally, no one in his right mind would've gone to him for help. I had to because I was broke. So a lack of cash, sometimes called Fate, had chosen him to become my personal physician.

"All right, Mr. Norber, what's your trouble?" he asked as he motioned to me a chair.

"I have a psycho-genic ailment that originated in service, which means I'm paranoid," I replied as I sat down.

He sat staring for a moment, blowing smoke at the chart on the desk. Then he looked up.

"Paranoid!" he exclaimed. "Izzat the pitch you're gonna use to get out'a the winter cold into this cozy tax-supported V.A. hospital?"

"Huh??? Yes, uh, no, but..." I stammered. I was dumbfounded! Yes, I meant I felt paranoid, yes, the weather was cold, but I suffered no phobias of St. Louis winters, and spending time in a locked up psycho ward wasn't my idea of anything cozy.

"Some pitch!" I exclaimed. "What I'm leaving now, my loving wife and children, my home, what could be cozier than that?"

"All right, then, what makes you think you're paranoid?" he snapped.

"Because strange and unique things happen to me."

"And you feel you're unique," he interrupted.

I nodded and managed a "yes." I must've had an alarmed look, because of his abrupt manner. A look he misinterpreted.

"All right, Norber," he started again, his eyes boring through me, "just in case you get any wild ideas in your head, I suggest you get up and peek around the corner into the next room."

I walked to the doorway of an adjoining room. All I saw was a tall black attendant in a white uniform. "Nothing unusual about that," I thought as I returned to my chair.

"He can handle you, Norber," the doc ranted. "He's powerful and well-trained, so don't think you can jump me."

"You flatter me, Doc," I said, "but you are sure *you're* well?"

At that he leaned back in his chair halfheartedly smiling and sighing, assured that I was nonviolent.

Two seconds of silence.

"Would you believe, Mr. Norber, a patient tried to strangle me last week?" asked the doctor.

"Of course I'd believe it," I replied and haltingly added, "perhaps that's why you're feeling so insecure right now."

Dr. Gilpin smiled. "It sure helps to have the understanding of my patients."

"Thanks," I smiled in return, as I settled more comfortably in my chair, satisfied rapport had been established.

"Now that you're comfortable," said Gilpin, noting my ease, "tell me something unique that's happened to you."

"Well, what I have in mind is a story that began in World War II, I could make it brief..."

"So go ahead," snapped Gilpin, "I'm used to war stories – shoot!"

Briefly, I told Dr. Gilpin of Bill and his handicap of illiteracy and my writing letters for him. And then I told him what occurred in Indianola, Mississippi, very carefully pointing out that it was the first, last, and only time I'd ever set foot in Mississippi. I also indicated that I was some forty miles away from Bill's home town and I conjectured the Miz Aldy I spoke to I may very well have written.

"I'll give you that," Dr. Gilpin volunteered. "So you ran into someone you wrote letters to, what's so unique about that?"

Before I could even reply, Gilpin cut me off with "Lots of guys wrote letters for their illiterate buddies. You didn't do anything unusual!"

I started to protest. *"You missed the whole point,"* doctor, I asserted.

But my words were wasted. I might as well have been talking to the moon.

"Mr. Norber, do you know why you think your story is unique?"

"Because it is unique," I replied.

"Mr. Norber," said my doctor, his voice adopting an arbitrary authoritative ring, "I've got news for you. There's nothing unique about your story. You just think so because you're psycho, and believe me, you are psycho!"

I tried to explain the point. "But what about the odds," I insisted. "There are two million people in Mississippi."

I never finished.

The doctor had a way of changing a subject he didn't care to continue. "You know, Norber," he said, "you told me a story that went back all the way to World War II, and believe me, I've heard quite a few of them. Yours is not unique or noticeably different from others, but this I'll say – it wasn't a combat centered story. But," he added, "Maybe you and your outfit never knew about tough combat."

"Hurtgen Forest was tough," I replied.

"Hurtgen..." the doctor repeated, looking blankly at me, "I never heard of it."

The tall black attendant in the white uniform who had been waiting in the adjoining room now made his appearance.

Laying my medical records aside and turning to the attendant, the doctor said, "Would you show Mr. Norber our cozy quarters? He's going to be spending the winter with us."

THIS IS MEDICINE???

It appears to me that at best, the "head man" at any asylum hearing endless wild dreams, fantasies, and implausible stories, runs a grave risk of becoming a "case" himself. My doctor had taken that risk.

Dr. Gilpin was an interesting case. An emaciated, scarecrow-like stick figure of a man, medium height with a pasty-white face contoured by sunken cheeks, through which ran rivulets of nerves and involuntary twitchings; he was an etching of a strange sickness. That he was ill was apparent, but that his illness could prevent him from properly understanding and performing medical duties was not apparent.

Having read my medical record, he should have known this: in the spring of 1954 when I was courting Jo, I suffered from an intracranial pressure that broke the blood vessels behind my eyes (at the fundus). Spinal taps administered by non-V.A. physicians had remedied the physical condition, but the pressure on my brain had been extreme; my thinking became confused. The neurologist treating me recognized the symptoms. He advised me to go to the V.A. and tell them I had a "psychogenic" ailment that originated in service and should be hospitalized. I was then hospitalized for about one year, during which time my treatment consisted mainly of rest and relaxation. No drugs or shock treatment of any type were ever used. I was released in a good state of remission.

Despite the fact that Dr. Gilpin had read my record, he erroneously believed I had been given the drug 'Thorazine' as treatment in my previous hospitalization. Because of this error, I was to become far sicker from the drugs he prescribed than when I entered the hospital.

Following my admitting interview with Dr. Giltpin, I was shown to a couch in the dayroom. Presently a nurse appeared and handed me a small paper cup with a pill in it. I looked at the pill, shook my head no, and explained that I wasn't going to take any medicine. The nurse didn't quite see it that way. After a brief argument she turned on her heels and headed into Gilpin's office.

Dr. Gilpin now appeared, flanked by two attendants, and demanded that I swallow the pill. Another argument ensued. Soon Dr. Gilpin was raising his voice, proclaiming, "I prescribed this medicine and you are going to take it!"

In response I asked him several times what the name of the medicine was. And in replying to this, he insisted it was none of my business what it was; it was prescribed to help me get well.

While he was pressuring me I looked closely at the pill. The initials imprinted on the pill, SKF, reminded me of a somewhat similar looking pill that had been prescribed for me prior to my coming to the V.A. Hospital. The previous pill, Parnate, also had the imprint SKF on it. It had been prescribed by my private physician to lessen intracranial pressure. So, thinking this V.A. offering was Parnate in a different dosage, I ended the argument by popping the pill in my mouth and swallowing it.

At first I wasn't aware I was losing my mind; a severe depression began to come over me and I found myself walking around the ward crying without reason. Then things started taking on a strangeness I'd never known before. I started slipping out of contact with reality, my mind was becoming foggy and strange thoughts were starting to control me.

I spent the morning or afternoon of the first fog wandering down the corridor of the ward, smiling occasionally, maybe to someone, maybe not, but definitely not speaking to anyone. I didn't speak because I felt mute, unable to make words. While gripped by this feeling, a hand appeared and led me into a room and I heard a voice say, "Mr. Norber, you're supposed to join the discussion in the group therapy room today." (What could be more logical?) Feeling unable to speak, I sat in a stupor listening to everybody else. All I knew was everybody else was able to make words, what are words? One thought in particular kept circling through my head: *"Man, what great men are assembled here.* Listen to them make words, beautiful, brilliant words!" What they were talking about and whether they made sense didn't matter. *"They made words, and, by gosh, they belonged in Washington, D.C. Yes, they should be running the government!"*

Shortly after the group therapy meeting, Dr. Gilpin told me he wasn't satisfied with my progress, so he was ordering the Thorazine discontinued. But in its place would be a stronger drug: Stellazine. With the Stellazine my descent into a drugged hell was speeded up. Where once there was a ray of hope, soon there was none. Without warning, the light shut out completely, darkness covered my mind, and whatever was left of me was filled with feelings of guilt, depression and fear, and finally, compulsions of suicide.

It was a nice day for most of our ward's patients, and they were outside playing ball. Because of my behavior, I was not allowed to participate in activities. Our ward was to be closed for the afternoon so I was transferred to the locked ward located directly across the hall.

I was dragging through the corridor of that ward in the direction of an unlocked secluded room which was being painted, and in which there was a screen less, open window. The woman psychiatrist who ran this ward interrupted my stroll and directed me into the dayroom. No trouble, my compulsion had to be satisfied. I had some car keys I'd managed to obtain, tried fitting them in the electrical outlet in the wall of the dayroom.

Now the doors to my home ward were reopened, and I was returned there and immediately put in seclusion under the care of a watchful attendant. For many days I was fogged up; mentally in and out of contact and physically in and out of seclusion. On my better days, when the fog wasn't too heavy, I was allowed to leave the seclusion area to roam about through the ward, but always I was kept under the eyes of the watchful attendant; and he watched as I unscrewed light bulbs from various floor lamps and inserted my fingers into the empty sockets. In a way I had my own personal electric shock treatments. The siege of this madness was interrupted by something even worse: the worst physical ailment I have ever known, "the perpetual motion syndrome."

This can only be described by saying my body was driven by an uncontrolled force that set me into motion which I could not stop; I was driven into fits of prolonged walking. In addition, there were other times my body was forced into spells marked by continuous physical activity. Afflicted in this manner, I was unable to voluntarily sit down, lie down, or relax for more than a few minutes without being driven upright by this force that propelled me into prolonged walking.

For days I paced the corridors endlessly, my leg muscles cramping and my body aching from fatigue. At night when I tried to lie in bed, I had to keep rolling from side to side, to keep moving, unable to stop until I was parched and dry and my tongue would stick to the roof of my mouth and I would drift off into an exhausted sleep period of some few hours.

At that time I did not know that these actions were all part of a syndrome that is a side effect peculiar to the drug Stellazine, and is medically referred to as "extra-pyramidal effects." My doctor didn't know about this medical reference either, so he insisted I take this drug. The drugs were now wrecking me physically as well as mentally, but my doctor kept a stiff upper lip; he was not discouraged.

One day after repeated requests, I was allowed an audience with Dr. Gilpin. He sat at his desk staring at me while I stood trembling, shifting from one foot to the other.

"The drugs are causing this," I said, referring to my actions.

"Sit down, Mr. Norber!"

I sat, but had to rise immediately.

"Sit down, Mr. Norber!"

I tried a second time and had to get up immediately again. Shifting and tottering, I blurted, "You're wrecking me with the Stellazine!"

"Sit down, Mr. Norber!"

I tried a third time, and fortunately I managed to seat myself long enough to present my case. I argued strongly that the drugs were having an adverse effect on me.

He tossed aside my argument by saying that I had previously been hospitalized in 1954, at which time I had been successfully treated with Thorazine.

To this I objected. "I was ill in 1954, true, but I didn't take Thorazine or any other drug."

"Mr. Norber," he responded, "on your previous hospitalization you were here for quite some time, and during that time you were successfully treated with Thorazine."

"Oh, no," I said. "It's true I was here for approximately a year, from 1954 to 1955, but I took no drugs, and if you knew my medical record you'd know that."

That upset him. "I know your medical record and you were on Thorazine!" He enunciated his words slowly and deliberately.

"Doctor," I replied, "in the spring of 1954 I had an intracranial pressure that led to my being hospitalized here. My treatment here consisted mainly of rest and recreation. No drugs or shock treatment of any sort were used at any time during my entire stay."

In reply he arched his eyebrows.

I shouted at the eyebrows, "I never had any medicine of any sort!"

With that he got up and went to the file for my record. "Now I'll prove you're wrong," he said, "and that will settle it!" Returning to his chair with my folder, he leaned back, opened the folder, and started his review. After several minutes thumbing through the record, it became apparent he wasn't finding what he was looking for, but he was not to be denied.

"Aha!" he suddenly cried, "here's an entry that shows you took a bicarbonate of soda.."

"*A bicarbonate of soda?*" I repeated. "Well, yes, I remember I once had an upset stomach during that year so I asked for a "bicarb," but that's not Thorazine or the kind of drugs we are talking about."

"But you said you took no medicine," he countered.

Because the peculiar doctor-patient relationship we had demanded that the patient is always wrong, I let him have the last word.

Then he tried another tack. "Mr. Norber, do you recognize you're sick?"

"Yes."

"Do you want to be cured?"

"Yes."

"Do you know how tobacco is cured?"

"No."

"Then I'll tell you this much, the cure takes time. The treatment given the tobacco has to work its way completely through the leaves. If it's to be effective, the cure has to work its way through all the cells of the leaves, and that takes time and patience. It's the same way with your cure." And all the time he spoke, he exhaled his words through a thick blanket of cigarette smoke.

I could sit still no longer. Unable to contain myself, I bolted from my chair and started into my dance. "May I be excused now?"

"Yes," he said, but trust me. I'm a doctor and I know what I'm talking about."

Back in the corridors I started pacing. I could feel the nervous tremors running up and down the calves of my legs, tremors that could never be cured. My fingers trembled so badly I could hardly place a handkerchief to my nose when needed; I was being cured. My mind was fast becoming a blur again. The combination of the drugs and the doctor were too much for me.

A small group of aides, nurses and attendants, stood in a cluster outside the doctor's office. I went to them. "Is Dr. Gilpin a doctor? I mean, is he an M.D.?"

"What kind of question is that?" asked one of the attendants. "Is the doctor a doctor, of course, he's a doctor. He wouldn't be here if he wasn't."

"But is he a psychiatrist?" I demanded.

"Mr. Norber, you're all worked up. Dr. Gilpin is a good doctor. He knows what he's doing. Trust him."

I walked away. *"I guess they're right; I'm all worked up. Not trusting the doctor was just another symptom of my paranoia."*

My pace in the corridor quickened. Somebody tapped me on the shoulder. I turned and saw "Stubby," a short, chubby little fellow-patient friend of mine.

"Did you see the doctor about your pill, that little blue pill?" he asked.

"Yes, and I'm being cured," I replied.

Stubby shook his head. "No, no you're not; you're getting worse. I know. I've been on that pill, too, and I know what it does to you." Then he continued, "Did you ever try to kill yourself?"

"Yes."

"So did I," said Stubby. "I tried to drown myself in a tub of water, but they caught me. It was the pill, the little blue pill. Don't take it. Put in your mouth, pretend, but don't swallow it."

"But you don't understand," I replied. "I haven't tried to kill myself lately. The worst is all behind me now. Now I'm really being cured. All I need is endurance; a little patience and I'll be completely cured."

There was an odd comfort in what Stubby had said about his suicide attempt. He had acted on a suicidal compulsion and survived. I wondered if perhaps we had shared other common experiences.

"Did you ever go deaf?" I asked. "Did you ever watch people moving their lips, know that they're talking, but you can't hear because you're stone deaf?"

"No", said Stubby, "never had that one. Can't say I ever heard of that one before."

"Well, I'm past that, too," I beamed. "I'm being cured liked tobacco."

Stubby looked at me oddly, scratched his head and walked away.

I spent the next couple of days in seclusion, enduring; however, my attendant wasn't enduring. Having tired of screwing in light bulbs around the ward, and now wearied of watching my frenzied pace, he placed a call to the doctor who was on duty for the day in place of Gilpin.

On observing me, this doctor recognized that I was suffering from the extra-pyramidal side effects of Stellazine, so he ordered a "cutter" drug, Cogentun, to eliminate these side effects.

Shortly after taking the Cogentun pill, the uncontrollable force that drove me into perpetual motion suddenly stopped. Like a balloon that has been punctured and floats to the ground, so did I settle onto a chair. For the first time in days I knew what it was to sit down and relax. I was hurt and aching and totally exhausted, but very relieved. After resting in the chair for a rather long period, I felt confident that I was in control again. I moved to my cot and stretched my body out full length and just relaxed and felt good all over. The worst physical torment I had ever known, even exceeding those of World War II, had come to an abrupt end.

The next day Dr. Gilpin returned to the ward and an attendant told me he wanted to see me in his office. What he had to say didn't take long; only that I would no longer take Stellazine.

The Stellazine horror was over and everything started to take a turn for the better. A physical examination revealed I was in need of some minor surgery, so I was sent to the surgical ward. This, of course, meant I was removed from Dr. Gilpin, and this in turn improved my mental outlook.

Probably because of overcrowding in Dr. Gilpin's admitting ward, my return there was delayed and my stay in the surgical ward was lengthened. For about a month I enjoyed the freedom of this ward, and it was a welcome respite. When I was finally transferred back to the admitting ward, I was so markedly improved that I was quickly transferred to Dr. Gilpin's open ward. Here everything and everybody seemed friendly. Even my interviews with Dr. Gilpin took on a different tone. The atmosphere in his office, though hazy, was warm and for the first time I was able to see him in a different light. He was human.

Physically he had not changed. He was still a walking wreck of skin and bones beset by tremors from head to foot. Mentally, he was always preoccupied with thoughts of his patients. Watching him hurrying through his morning rounds I could conclude only that he had a great deal of zeal and good intentions. He made errors and serious ones could not be denied. Yet he was very seriously a dedicated person. Any man who had been physically attacked by violent patients, and, on one occasion, almost strangled to death, and still continues to serve those patients to the best of his abilities, is quite a man. That he was a born fighter who had taken too many punches and was fighting a losing fight was obvious.

It's a curious thing that a sick patient on the mend sometimes can discern a sickness in a physician when one exists, so there was nothing too unusual in my being able to see that Dr. Gilpin was sick. Moreover, I was not the only patient who recognized his condition.

It was during an informal discussion in his office when we were exchanging views on things we liked to do for enjoyment, that I caught a glimpse of his human side.

"Sometimes," he said, leaning back in his chair, "I feel like I'd just like to sit back on a fishing bank and spend the rest of my life fishing for bluegill. Now there's the life." For a moment he seemed to stare far out into nowhere, almost to dream. Then he caught himself. "Do you ever fish, Norber?"

He'd even forgotten to say "Mr.", and I could see he was talking to me as a friend.

"No," I replied, "fishing's not for me. I'd take golf, but you know, the warm weather is with us again and you oughta think about going fishing."

"A good idea," he said. "I'll think about it."

"Why just think about it? Why not really go out, get away from here for a while, and really enjoy yourself?"

I knew he was going downhill. His fingers were becoming more and more tremulous, and tremors raced more often through his sunken cheekbones. His face had the sick hollow look of a man who's been warmed over by death. But his voice was strong. He understood what I was driving at.

"And if I were to leave this place, who would look after these veterans?"

At a previous time had he asked this question, I would have answered him differently. But now that I knew him better, I could only say, "Well, doctor, try not to knock yourself out."

When the patient starts understanding the doctor's problems, he's on the way out. And for me there was a way out, but for Dr. Gilpin there seemingly was none. His physical and mental health shot through, his abilities as a doctor faded; he had lost the battle and didn't know it. (Certainly it came as no surprise to me when much later, after I was discharged, I heard that he had suffered a nervous breakdown, and was hospitalized as a psychiatric patient.)

The summer of 1963 was a time of slow recovery for me. Weekdays I spent confined to the hospital premises, but weekends found me home on trial visits with my family. For my family, my wife and three little children, it was a trying time. Quite naturally, my states of anxiety and changing moods were unexplainable to the children, but my wife understood. And because of her patience and understanding, the atmosphere in our home, while not entirely friction free, was nevertheless far more comforting than that of the wards. With each trial visit I seemed to improve. My stay at the hospital was coming to an end.

One early morning in the fall or winter of 1963, I stood facing Dr. Gilpin in his office for the last time. I recall it was early in the morning, for I could see the doctor's features clearly; an unopened pack of cigarettes was on his desk; the blue haze had not yet started. After a customary exchange of pleasantries, the doctor handed me my diploma, a discharge slip from the hospital stating I had received "maximum hospital benefits."

I was going home.

HOME AGAIN

My decision in January of 1963 to leave my wife and young children, the warmth and comfort of home, to enter a V.A. hospital had been a difficult one forced on me by recurrence of the illness that had originated in an Army snake pit during World War II.

At the onset of the recurred illness, late in 1962, I had returned to the neurologist who had previously treated me in 1954. Had I been able to afford private treatment, I would have remained in his care. However, as I was not, and since the ailment had originated in service, the only recourse left to me was the Veterans Administration.

Leaving home to enter a V.A. hospital was like having my heart ripped out, but it had to be done. So it was a miserable morning when I kissed my wife, two small daughters and one small son goodbye, promised them I'd be gone for "only a little while", and departed.

I never realized that "only a little while" would mean almost a year. But now that year was past and everything that happened during that period was all behind me. The only thing that mattered to my family and me was that I was coming home!

Our home and hearth was an apartment building in a somewhat rundown section of a wealthy suburb. I'll always remember the day I returned there. The door to the living room of our apartment opened and I stood looking into the sparkle of two lovely luminous green eyes: the same green eyes that had lured me from confirmed bachelorhood to the altar on New Year's Day, 1956. Now, seven years and three children later, the light in her eyes and the look in her lovely face were the same as they were when we had taken each other "for better or worse."

The past year for her couldn't have been an easy one. On her alone had fallen the responsibility of rearing our children and keeping our home intact. Being of a patient and tender nature, she is a beautiful mother, but more than that, in keeping our home together, she had shown a maturity normally considered far beyond her years.

Jo is twelve years younger than I, and blessed with a face of classic beauty. Behind her beautiful light green wide-spaced eyes there is a mind that is rich in understanding.

When I first took notice of her back in the days when we were both unattached and living in the same neighborhood, I was well aware of her youth and charm, but hadn't particularly noticed her mind. And even if I had, it is doubtful that anything like a woman's mind could have lured me from my established bachelorhood. As a man already in my early thirties, I knew one thing for certain: I'd live and die a bachelor. Marriage was not for me. And I felt that way right up until the moment I first saw her.

Looking back, I can see that our marriage was based on more than just physical attraction. We shared enough things in common, we believed, to give our marriage a firm footing. Despite our so-called cultural differences, our values and goals in life were alike, and although we were of different religions, we were of the same faith. So, aside from the evident fact that she is beautiful and I love beauty, there was good reason to believe we could share a life together.

Our first six years saw our home blessed with three lovely children. In caring for them, Jo and I felt the heartaches and joys that most parents feel during their children's early years. In sharing these feelings, it was only natural that we as parents grew in our love and respect for each other. Neither of us could imagine our home without the presence of the other.

So, it was a shocking thing that hit our household late in 1962, late in the seventh year of our marriage, when I suddenly became ill and had to be hospitalized.

At that time the first shock Jo faced was not only my being hospitalized, but the manner of hospitalization. Her first visit to me as a patient in a locked ward in a mental institution had been an eye-opener. She did not comprehend the need for my being locked up (and for that matter, neither did I), nor did she understand why she was not allowed to speak with my doctor. (Fortunately, she had been unable to visit me during the Stellazine episode and so was spared that shock.)

At home her efforts to provide for the security of our family were complicated and seriously hampered by a critical shortage of funds. Borrowed money put milk and bread on the table. So the year had been an ordeal for her, too.

To pick up the threads of life again and to provide for the happiness of my loved ones meant not only to reenter the mainstreams of family and social life, but the economic ones as well. Since I had previously worked in the back office of a stockbroker, I had no difficulty obtaining work with another brokerage firm. My former experience while essential in getting the new job, proved useless in helping me to adjust to my new working conditions, for I was no longer my former self. Despite my firm resolve that I would succeed in making everything work out, it seemed that from the very beginning nothing did. In a matter of a few months I felt myself slipping back into a mental rut. I believed I needed another type of job. With this in mind, I took a day off to take a civil service exam.

When I got the civil service job it was classified as "temporary." But I took it as a breather, hoping to follow it up with something permanent in civil service. The breather, however, turned out to be no different from my previous job because I was still sick, and getting sicker. After a few months the job terminated. Having done my best and failed, I felt terminated too.

At about this time, the V.A. somehow came to the conclusion that my condition wasn't good, and they advised that for the time being I should not consider working. At their recommendation I retired to my home.

WE DINE AT THE RITZ IN MISSISSIPPI

For a period of six years a condition of general uneasiness prevailed in our home. Many times during those years, Jo, not liking the unhealthful atmosphere, suggested that what we needed most was a good vacation. I agreed, but with my limited understanding of arithmetic and bank balances, I didn't see how we could afford it.

But this one particular May morning in 1970 I was feeling totally defeated and was brooding over breakfast when "Green Eyes," looking very brilliant and beautiful, sat down across the table from me. It was obvious she knew something I didn't know.

"We're going to Florida," she said, handing me a stack of pamphlets and literature she'd been receiving from various chambers of commerce and resort places located there. "All you have to do is choose one," she added.

"Okay, I'll go along with it," I said, if you can explain your figures, or is it new math?"

"Simple," she said. "New math, as you call it, is the theory that all patriotic Americans must subscribe to in our society in order to keep our economy functioning. I'm referring of course, to credit financing." Then she laid one charge plate on the table. "We'll use this."

In order to prove my patriotism and to keep our economy from malfunctioning, I agreed to help plan our vacation.

Several months later, in August 1970, under the sponsorship of "Mastercharge," our family departed from the St. Louis area bound for the vacation land of our dreams: Ft. Walton Beach, Florida. This was to be our first vacation in almost 14 years.

Grenada, Mississippi, is about the half-way mark on our trip, and it was there we decided to stop after the first day's travel. After a good night's rest at a motel, we pulled out early in the morning, skipping breakfast, hoping to hit the highway at its least congested hour in order to make good time. We hadn't traveled too far, however, before we hit a stretch of extremely bumpy road. The narrow highway into Durant, Mississippi, was pockmarked by chuckholes. Dodging and bouncing along that road didn't help my coffee–less disposition. On top of that, Jo and the children were getting hungry.

As we drove through the streets of Durant I heard the children's voices blending in harmony in one appeal: "Food, we need food, we're hungry!" Next came, "If you don't feed us soon, we'll all starve right here in Mississippi, and all the people down here won't like you, Yankee." I drove on. Finally, the youngest one's cry that always gets me "I think I'm gonna be sick!"

I looked alarmingly at Jo opposite me on the front seat. Wisely we started a sharp look-out for a restaurant or cafe. After driving around the town square a couple of times and seeing none, I suggested that we go on to the next town. But the cries and groans of hunger from the back seat became disturbingly worse. Unable to spot an eating place, I pulled over the side of the first filling station I came to, and asked the attendant if he knew where a restaurant was located.

"Why, you've pulled up right to it," he said, pointing to a sign in the window of the store which was standing in back of the filling station. The sign in the window read, "The Ritz Cafe."

We dragged into the cafe and were promptly met by a sweet middle-aged waitress who seated us at a table and handed us menus.

My head seemed to clear and my eyes opened with the first cup of coffee. Suddenly a thought struck me: "How far could Sallis be from here?" I remembered writing letters to someone in Durant.

The waitress had just finished refilling my cup with fresh coffee when I looked up at her and asked, "Could you tell me how far Sallis, Mississippi is from here?"

The waitress met my question with a hard stare. "What do you want to know for?"

I was baffled by the directness of her question. "Well," I smiled in a friendly manner, "I used to know someone from Sallis."

"Who did you know from Sallis?" she asked.

I realized I must've appeared to her to be a prying outsider or maybe worse, a snooping "revenoo-er." "Well, it was a long time ago, back in World War II," I said.

"What was his name?" she asked.

"Bill Aldy," I replied, "he..."

"Bill Aldy!" she exclaimed, her eyes wide as saucers. "He was my cousin, my favorite cousin. You knew Bill? You were with him??"

My wife and I sat stunned. The atmosphere seemed electric.

Jo had heard the Indianola story many times before. Now she sat looking at me. "You're psychic, Vic," she said.

I knew she was mistaken, for in no way did I suspect or anticipate this happening. "I'm not psychic," I said, "I'm shocked."

It was incredible. Twice in my life I had entered the state of Mississippi and twice in my life I asked a simple question, "Where is Sallis located?"

Our waitress immediately transformed herself into a warm, friendly person, and we broke into animated conversation revolving around Bill. Naturally I told her first what a fine soldier he was. Before I knew it, we were wrapped up in an exciting exchange. Because of this, we failed to introduce ourselves, but for the time being this made no difference. In talking about Bill and his native intelligence, I very carefully made no mention of his illiteracy. I wanted her to know I knew him well enough to be considered a good friend, so I recalled the names of his brothers, Guy and Aubrey, saying I knew these because Bill and I, being members of the same tank crew, often spoke of our families.

As we talked on, I related how Bill's good nature had made him many friends. At this, she seemed pleased and proud. "You know," she said, recalling the time long past, "I remember how good he was about writing, well, you see, he wrote me occasionally, but he wrote my daughter more regularly."

Our talk suddenly ended. The proprietor of the restaurant glanced our way. Other customers were waiting to be served. The waitress, realizing this, reluctantly excused herself and left to serve the other customers. As soon as she was gone, Jo and I discussed the strangeness of this coincidence. As we were finishing breakfast, I explained to Jo that the few minutes I had talked with Bill's cousin just wasn't enough for me, that too much had been left unsaid.

I wanted to level with Bill's cousin, let her know I really remembered the names of Bill's brothers from having personally written Bill's letters. I also wanted her to know I knew of his family in another way from having read their letters to him. She'd understand why I'd said nothing about this before.

Before leaving, the restaurant I saw her standing alone behind a counter. I walked over to her. We spoke in lowered tones. In resuming our conversation, I told her of my meeting the Aldy woman in Indianola. "That Aldy," she said, "had married another cousin of Bill's and had moved from Sallis to Indianola. "She wasn't actually blood kin to Bill." In speaking of Bill's family, I learned that one of the brothers had died and that at present time his father was sick.

When I said I was sorry to hear the misfortune that had hit the Aldy family, she looked straight into my eyes. "I know Bill had a lot of friends, but seeing that you even remembered the names of those in his family, I believe you must have been a really close friend of his. I know it sure would make his folks feel good if you would visit with them."

At this point, I let her know that I had personally handled all of Bill's correspondence and because of that I recalled the names of those in his family.

"Then you will go visit them?" she asked. "It's only six miles up the road, and I know they'd be so happy talking about the things we talked of."

"It's been a long time, over twenty-five years." (Inwardly I wondered if barging in on them, especially with illness in the family, might make matters worse). "Tell you what," I said, "on our way back from Florida, I'll stop by and see them."

Assured of that, she changed the subject. "You know, before, over at the table, I mentioned that my daughter and I heard from Bill. Now from what you told me that means you wrote the letters to us, too?"

"Yes, that's right," I replied, and in the back of my mind wheels were turning. I was standing there thinking, recalling. Then I had it! The name of the people I wrote to here in Durant. It wasn't too uncommon; their name was Culpepper, so now I decided to wait until we were through talking this time. Then I'd surprise her by letting her know I remembered her name also.

As our conversation was drawing to a close, and as I was turning to leave, I hesitated for a moment, then turned back to her and said, knowingly, "You might find this a little unusual, but I recall the name of the people I wrote to here in Durant."

"You do?" she replied. "And what was their name?"

"Culpepper," I smiled. "Their name was Culpepper."

"Culpepper," she repeated. "Oh, she owns the other restaurant at the other end of the block."

At this I blinked. Then, not knowing what to say, I hurried on to join Jo and the children who were waiting for me at the door of the restaurant.

As we walked out into the bright clear morning air, I stood still for a moment, perplexed, trying to collect my thoughts. Let's see, now, *This is the second time I've been in Mississippi, and each time I've run into a unique situation relating to Bill Aldy, and this time between two restaurants, and in each restaurant someone I'd written to for Bill. Hmmmmmm.*

As our car pulled away from the Ritz Cafe, I told Jo of my conversation with our waitress. In explaining my view of the present situation, I referred to it as "unique."

"Be careful of that word 'unique,'" Jo cautioned. "Remember Dr. Gilpin."

We both laughed, remembering the hang-up Gilpin and I had had over the use of the word "unique". And I, being one who not easily forgets medical wrong doings, turned suddenly serious, and I flared, "That man was wrong, then, one hundred percent wrong!!" And if this repeat visit to Mississippi proves anything, it proves that psychiatric arbiter was one hundred percent wrong!"

Somewhere beyond the blue, somewhere in endless space, I could imagine hearing a friendly voice chuckling, "I'll guaran-cotton-pickin'-tee ya you're right, ole buddy.".......Only he didn't say cotton-pickin'."

WHAT GOES AROUND...

Floating in the ocean's surf on air cushioned rafts and romping around and relaxing on a white sandy beach were forms of enjoyment our land-locked family had never before experienced. Fort Walton Beach, Florida, was proving to be the perfect tonic for our family's needs. For five or six days all we knew was luxurious living and fun on the beach.

And then, as the first week of our vacation drew to a close, the tonic suddenly ran out. That is, we all became severely sunburned. So, in the last week, we knew no tonic – only lotions. Plenty of lotions.

When the morning finally came for us to leave Florida to start on our homeward journey, we weren't too unhappy to say goodbye to the beach. Being extremely sore from our sunburns we all felt that our trip home should be made in a leisurely manner, in order not to tax our strength. The only out of the way stop we planned to make was the Aldy home.

So it was the second morning of our homeward journey that found us on that lonely black-topped country road in Mississippi – a road I'd looked forward to traveling down with great anticipation, the road that led to Sallis, Bill's home.

The windows in the car were all lowered and the morning air blowing through the car felt refreshing and cooling to our sunburned faces. The green fields on either side of the road were fresh and alive and glistening with dew. And sometimes, looking out into the fields, it seemed I could see forever. The horizon appeared far away, and as far as the eye could see, there appeared endless expanses of green ridges and low slanting green hills. And here and there little forests of green trees sprang up first in the background and then coming closer to the highway, shortening the view.

Crossing a small bridge, I could hear the trickle of a nearby stream and I was thinking to myself, *this must have been Bill's playground....* As if in harmony with my thoughts Jo was saying, "I can see why Bill loved to spend his days out here exploring and running through the fields, instead of sitting in a classroom. It's so beautiful here." At that moment, in my imagination, I could see Bill as a boy, barefoot and with a fishing pole, running in and out among the trees looking for a good fishing bank.

My thoughts wandered from Bill back to the present, and I thought of meeting his mother, the one whose letters I'd read so many times a quarter of a century earlier. She'd be along in years now, no doubt elderly looking, and her face would be gentle.

The sign on the road "Sallis, Mississippi" roused me from my thoughts.

A short distance ahead, sitting at the bottom of a hill, was a gas station. I pulled into the station and asked the attendant if he knew where the home of Mrs. W. C. Aldy might be.

"Frame house on the left at the top of the hill."

We drove up the hill and when we reached the house, I pulled into the driveway. Leaving Jo and the children in the car, I went to the house and knocked on the front door. No answer. I knocked again, this time louder. Still no answer. She had to be home, or at least nearby, I hoped. I left the front of the house and walked alongside it, past my car in the driveway, toward the backyard. "Anybody home?"

"Hello there, lookin' for someone?" A large man in overalls appeared in the backyard.

"Is this the home of Mrs. W. C. Aldy?" I asked.

"It sure is, and I'm her son."

Before the man went further I spoke up, giving him my name and saying I had been a friend of Bill's in the Army during the War, and I was stopping by to see his mother. Then I asked, "Is your mother home?"

Responding first to my introduction, the man said, "My name's Frank (a name I didn't recognize). Bill was my half-brother." Then, answering my question, he said, "Mom's in town, no tellin' when she'll be back; could be sometime late this afternoon, no tellin'." Then, glancing at the car in the driveway, he stated, "If you and your folks care to stay a bit we could talk, or maybe you could come back later."

Thanking Frank for his invitation, I explained my family's situation to him, saying that my wife and children were all terribly sunburned, and because of their condition, we couldn't wait or come back later. Then, thinking a picture is worth a thousand words, I raised a pant leg, showing Frank a badly sunburned leg.

"Good Lord!" he exclaimed, "That is one terrible burn."

Walking back to the car with me, Frank said, "Mom will be real sorry she missed you. She sure would'a been glad to talk to with you."

As we started pulling out of the driveway, I said, "I'll be sure to drop a line when I get home."

"You do that, please. I'm sure she'd like to hear from you."

And that's all there was to the visit. So it hadn't been in the cards for me to see Mrs. Aldy.

I had been very disappointed in not seeing Bill's mother, whom I'd seen so many times in my imagination. Recalling that I had skipped visiting her on our way down to Florida because the waitress in the Ritz Cafe in Durant said Bill's father was sick, I suppose Fate had determined that I wasn't to meet Bill's mother; that my contact with her was supposed to be limited to letters.

One of the first things I did after our return home was to write Bill's mother. I wasn't too concerned over what I would write, because I felt she'd appreciate anything I wrote about her son. In my letter I told her about the crap games Bill and I had been in together, and how he was the one man who would never bet against me. Unbelievably, I wrote of crap games, of all things, to show her how much the idea of friendship meant to Bill; that Bill was one of my best friends. *What was I thinking?!*

A day or two after I mailed the letter I started to have misgivings. Had I chosen an inappropriate topic? Had I done wrong? Had I said something that could be misconstrued? I was sorry I'd ever mentioned crap games.

My worry about this was short-lived, however, because several days after I'd mailed the letter I received her reply. When I opened the letter and saw her quaint and gentle salutation, I felt relieved. "Kind Sir," she greeted me. And then before I knew it I became lost in a simply worded, eloquent letter. A letter from a mother's heart about her son.

In speaking of Bill she wrote of his deeply generous nature; how as a young boy he had left school and gone to work as soon as he was old enough to work to help out at home because of "hard times" (something Bill had never told me). She recalled how as a generous child he shared whatever he earned, and then much later, when he was a grown man and out on his own, he sent her thirty dollars a week. And it was like she said: "He could do most any kind of work." And she wrote too of something that must have been comforting to her: that many of Bill's friends in service had written to her after his death. It was a letter of many good things I liked to read about. But her letter closed on a very sad note, "I have missed him so much."

I didn't want the letter to close on that note, so I returned to the body of the letter reading only the words between the opening and closing lines. And, in reading this way, over and over again, about this generous and outgoing son of hers, this beautiful lady was doing something only she could do. Something she had done many, many years ago when first she brought Bill into this world. She was, in the pages of her letter, bringing back into this world the spirit of her beloved son.

REUNION IN ST. LOUIS

The 5th Armored Division Association had recently notified me that a reunion of the division would be held at the Jefferson Hotel in Downtown St. Louis in July of 1950.

I received the notice with mixed emotions. I wanted to go to the reunion because I wanted to see some of my former buddies. But then, I didn't want to go because I was afraid I'd see someone I didn't want to see or someone would see me who didn't want to see me. Feelings of guilt and shame, memories of Bergstein still haunted me.

On the first morning of the reunion, I went to the Jefferson Hotel. I had been standing in the lobby milling around in the crowd for about a half-hour looking for a familiar face. Seeing none during that time, I was about to leave when out of the crowd emerged Rogers. He'd spotted me and was coming over to say hello. The last time I'd seen Rogers was when he leaped from the back deck of my tank and disappeared on a battlefield being saturated by German artillery. I was glad to see he was alive and well.

As we were happily greeting each other, we were joined by another familiar face, "Major Does-Less." With "Does-Less" were two of his buddies whom he promptly introduced to Rogers and me. For a few minutes our group of five stood in the lobby talking about our old Army days, when Rogers suggested that we all go out for coffee.

That sounded like a good idea, so we left the lobby and went to the Jefferson Coffee Shop next door where we got a table large enough to seat the five of us.

It was a while we were having coffee and doughnuts and "Does-Less" and his buddies were talking among themselves briefly that Rogers turned to me and said, "I was hoping you'd show up because I have something I wanted you to see."

"What is it?" I asked.

Before showing me what he wanted me to see he asked, "You're not a member of the Association, are you?"

"No, I'm not, but they somehow got my address and let me know about the reunion."

"I figured you weren't a member," Rogers said, "because I knew if you were you would have answered a notice that's appeared several times in the Association News." As he spoke, he reached into his wallet and withdrew a clipping he had taken from an edition of the 5th Armored News, and handed it to me.

The clipping read, "Would anyone knowing the circumstances of the death of my son, Joe Verhagen, killed in action Dec. 6, 1944 in Bergstein, Germany, please contact me?" Under the notice appeared Mrs. Verhagen's name and address.

"Didn't you write her?" I asked Rogers.

"No, I didn't," he replied.

"Well, why not?" I asked. "You were there when he was killed."

"Well, so were you," Rogers said. "You write her. I can't write a letter like that."

By "like that" I knew he meant a letter that would surely bring peace to the heart of Joe's mother, so without saying anything further, I took the clipping from Rogers and told him I would get a letter out to her as soon as I got home.

With that settled, we rejoined our friends in conversation.

After the coffee shop meeting broke up, I spoke privately with Rogers, telling him how glad I was to see him again and how thoughtful it was of him to bring me the clipping. Then we said goodbye.

On the bus home I started remembering Joe. Remembering him smiling, laughing at danger, seeing him playfully shaking his fist at me just before battle, saying, "I can whip 'em, can't we?" And then Bergstein where Rogers, who was in Joe's tank, said a hunk of shrapnel hit Joe in the head and he died instantly. Who could ever forget a guy like Joe? He was the most special person I'd ever known. Not only was he a credit to his family, his religion, and his community, but to the entire human race as well.

By the time I got home, writing the letter came easily.

A few days after I mailed the letter, I received the most sensitive and appreciative letter I'd ever had addressed to me. After telling me how grateful she was to get my most welcome letter, Mrs. Verhagen told of the pain she and her family felt on receiving the news of Joe's death on December 21, 1944. The Christmas season of '44 had been a time of great sorrow for the Verhagen family.

Though almost six years had passed since Joe's death and the pain she felt at the time had diminished, I could feel in reading her letter that she had received a great deal of comfort in hearing that her son had been killed instantly, without ever knowing what hit him.

In closing her letter, she extended a warm invitation to me and whatever family I might have, "little ones too," to visit her in the near future.

Though I never made it to Wisconsin, Mrs. Verhagen and I remained in touch with each other for the next thirty-five years by exchanging Christmas cards on which each of us wrote a little personal note. In her card of 1982, Mrs. Verhagen wrote that she had reached her 91st birthday and she still enjoyed reading the letter I sent regarding the loss of her son. At Christmas of 1984 I received a card from the Verhagen family telling me that Mrs. Verhagen was seriously ill and was receiving constant care from her family and a visiting nurse. Mrs. Verhagen passed away shortly thereafter.

Though I had never met Mrs. Verhagen, it seemed that I had known her personally because of our meaningful correspondence and long exchange of Christmas cards. Her letter in which she invited me and any family I might have to visit her is kept in my 5th Armored Division keepsake box.

Memories of World War II, especially those of combat, will remain forever implanted in my mind. The sense of guilt and shame I felt over having survived when so many others were killed or horribly mutilated or wounded will likewise remain with me throughout my life. Like thousands of other combat fatigue cases who share these same feelings of "survivor's guilt," I've learned to live with these feelings.

Along with the unpleasant memories and feelings I have retained from the war are also some very fond memories; memories of the fine men I was privileged to serve with and call my friends.

THE LETTER THAT BROUGHT US TOGETHER

Other than being Bastille Day, July 14 had no significant meaning to me, until the year 1954. It was on July 14, 1954, the temperature in St. Louis hit a record high of 115 degrees. While most of the city's inhabitants were sweltering in the heat, I felt like I was freezing as I sat on a bench in Forest Park, in the noon day sun, huddled in a fall sport coat, trying to get warm. The cold spell I was experiencing was an after-effect of a recent illness I had had, which affected my brain. From that day forward, July 14 would always have a certain meaning to me.

It was exactly forty-six years later, in the evening of July 14, 2000, while watching the television with my beautiful Commanding General, Jo, I wondered if the weatherman, in his nightly report, might allude to that day in our City's history, when the temperature soared to 115 degrees. While my stagnant mind was so preoccupied, the ringing of our telephone interrupted my thoughts.

Upon answering the phone, I heard the caller say, "Mr. Norber, you don't know me, but before I say anything else, I want to ask you, are you the Victor Norber who was in the 5th Armored Division during World War II, and did you know Joe Verhagen?"

I replied in the affirmative to both questions, and the caller then identified himself by name and the reason for his call. He said he was calling for Paul Verhagen, Joe's youngest brother. "Paul wants to meet you," he said. Then he continued, "Mr. Norber, a few years after the war ended, you wrote a letter to Joe's mother regarding Joe's death in a battle in Germany." I told him I remembered writing that letter. "Mr. Norber, that letter brought a good deal of comfort to Mrs. Verhagen and it was something she treasured." The caller further elaborated, "On many occasions, there would be a family gathering at her home in Kaukauna, and quite often on such occasions, Mrs. Verhagen would talk about her wonderful son, Joe, who had been killed in the war. And when she'd been talking about Joe, she would bring out your letter and read it aloud to all of the family, and then we'd all have a crying good time!"

The picture he described touched me. He informed me that Paul, his wife and their daughter and he would be on a road trip at the end of July and they would be in St. Louis on July 31. He asked if they could come visit me. "Yes," I said, "I feel honored. You set the time." We agreed on noon.

Precisely at noon on Sunday, July 31, our guests, Paul Verhagen and his wife Theresa arrived. With them were their married daughter Sara Weyenberg and her husband Pat, who initiated the phone call.

We greeted them with open arms; like family we hadn't seen in many years. After somewhat informal introductions, we seated ourselves in the living room. Before our conversation got underway, Paul arose from the sofa and handed me the letter I had written his mother a half century ago. I thanked him and laid the letter aside. I'd read it later.

We asked them questions about their trip. They said Kaukauna was 445 miles away and it had been a two-day trip because they traveled by daylight only and they traveled rather leisurely. They had left Kaukauna the previous afternoon, putting 300 miles behind them. They got a good meal and a good night's rest at a motel before covering the final 150 miles to St. Louis.

I asked our guests what brought them at this particular time to my doorstep. They indicated that July was the most convenient time for the family to vacation together and agreed to set aside time to honor the memory of Joe. They laid out an itinerary that would take them to places and people that meant so much to him during his lifetime.

The first stop was Bergstein in the Hurtgen Forest where Joe was killed. Next, they visited places in Germany and France, where Joe had fought. Last, they traveled to Holland, which suffered greatly during the war (the Verhagens were of Dutch descent). A very important place on their itinerary was my home to see Joe's buddy who knew him.

Without hesitation, I told them how I first met Joe, his bravery in battle and his generosity. I emphasized stories about his capabilities and the trust Captain Pool had in him. After talking continuously for a half hour, it dawned on me that I hadn't let Paul get in a word about his memories of Joe.

After telling us humorous anecdotes about his brother, Paul noted he didn't remember Joe that well because he was quite small when Joe went into the Army. He deferred to me. I returned to reminiscing about the best buddy I had ever known.

Sometimes when I paused to think, Jo would prompt me saying, "Tell them about the time...."

Once, I interrupted my monologue and asked them to tell me more about Joe, as they remembered him. "No, no," they exclaimed "You keep talking, you keep talking, we came to hear your stories, not ours." I continued telling seemingly endless stories until I glanced at my watch which told me it was time for a break.

Before we could serve refreshments, Pat opened his briefcase, containing photos of the large monument and museum the Germans had constructed in Bergstein honoring both the Germans and Americans who gave their lives in that horrible battle. While showing these photos, Pat took us inside the museum where we saw a written history and artifacts of that struggle. Paul interrupted momentarily to hand me pictures of Joe he knew I'd like to have. I gave Paul a copy of my memoirs.

With so much happening, Jo and I completely forgot it was time for refreshments. At my mention of food, the Verhagens said they came to hear my stories and not eat. They reminded us of their traveling schedule. Before leaving, Pat, knowing that I was sad to see them go, said they would be back sometime in the future. But I knew they wouldn't.

Around 3:00 p.m., we bid our friends a fond farewell and watched them as they drove away, heading home to Wisconsin. So ended a grand and glorious day.

I opened the envelope containing the letter I'd sent to Mrs. Verhagen in July 1950. I noticed the envelope was postmarked July 18, 1950. While reading the letter, I saw that I had dated my heading July 14, 1949. I was stunned. How could I have made such a stupid error?! From somewhere beyond the edges of space and the reach of time, I could hear a laughing voice, "Don't sweat it, Vic, you got the day right and for the year...well...You only missed it by one!"

July 14, 1949

Dear Mrs. Verhagen:

A friend of mine attending the 5th Armored Convention here in St. Louis first showed me an old news bit requesting to hear from anyone who knew your son, Joe.

I was Joe's gunner in all but his last battle. Putting last things first, I'll come right to the point on that in which you're most interested. Although I wasn't his gunner at Bergstein, I was commanding the tank next to his and know of his passing.

A great deal of artillery was bursting in the area when Joe's tank received a hit disabling it. He then ordered the tank abandoned. As he was getting to the ground a piece of shrapnel nicked his tank helmet. He never knew what hit him as he died instantly. His passing was painless and he was not disfigured. Given our circumstances and fate's calling, only the extremely good could have returned to our Maker in such a manner. This all occurred with such rapidity that there is just nothing else to write of it.

I hope it's proper to write more-about his life because I'd like to let you know what a fine man he was and why everyone was extremely fond of him. Although I may write of how I met and knew him, I'm speaking for everyone else as we all knew him to be the same.

I was out in California when I first met Joe. The thing that struck me immediately were his good looks and nature to match. I had never before run across such a good looking, good natured, unspoiled and wholesome creature in my life. I was not alone in my thoughts when I wished I could be in his tank crew.

From California, as you know, we went to Tennessee and from there to Pine Camp, N.Y. It was at Pine Camp that the lucky break came my way for I was transferred to his crew shortly after our arrival. I soon discovered that along with his good naturedness, several other ingredients were present. He had excellent mechanical abilities, a genuine common sense understanding of men, leadership qualities that were unexcelled, and an ever present sense of helpfulness.

Some of his favorite sayings typical of the underlying humor so prevalent in his speech, I'll never forget. One in particular he used when someone would "sidle up," to Joe and kiddingly say, "I'm gonna pin you ears back." Joe's casual reply was, "Well, don't let nothin' but fear stop you."

Joe's recounting of how he got his first black eye was also a jewel. He told me the story like this....He and another boy associated another twosome when the boy with Joe exclaimed, "I can whip 'em, can't we Joe?" Then Joe would conclude, "And that's how I got my first black eye." He used to come up to me with that good-humored twinkle in his eye and give out with his, "I can whip 'em, can't we, Vic?" Of course all he ever got out of me was a quizzical look wondering if he had the right party of the second part.

Among other things, Joe used to tell me of this brother, Mark, who was in the air corps, and after whom all German tanks were named. (Mark IV's, V's etc..etc.) You and yours and bits of his family life were always interesting. And oh yes, his girl friend Leona Van Gompel. His stories were always humorous and cheerful.

There was more to him than cheerfulness alone. I times of stress, his loyalty to a cause far greater than himself became evident. His acts of kindness were endless, and he was always humane all the way. To elaborate slightly on this note, I'd like to point to a small incident that happened in Bergstein.

A brief lull in the firing occurred during which a time a German infantryman suddenly appeared out of no-where waving a white cloth of surrender. Another tank commander near Joe was about to turn his machine gun on this enemy soldier when Joe yelled out to him, "Don't shoot, Van, he's surrendering." Joe was kind through and through, and had an ear for only kindness and loyalty, never hate.

One of the last fine mental pictures I have retained of Joe was formed slightly prior to our moving up. A fine drizzle had started to fall as he worked rapidly around the tank in his usual precise and constructive manner. For a moment as I watched him, I couldn't help thinking that here was the right hand of God. I'll never know a finer person.

"Helpful, brave, clean, kind,"--these were always the terms used when the fellows described Joe.

Well, Mrs. Verhagen, I'm sorry I didn't write you sooner, I should have done so years ago. I know I should have gotten your address before this, unfortunately I didn't receive the 5th Armored Division News.

I hope this letter finds you and yours in good health.

Very truly yours,

Vic Norber

316

Staff Sergeant Joseph Verhagen

Killed In Action December 6, 1944

Bergstein, Germany

Awarded posthumously Lieutenancy for Outstanding Leadership

and the Bronze Star for Valor

THE INVESTIGATION

8 November 1944

Somewhere in the Hurtgen Forest in Germany, in the well-concealed basement command post of General Norman D. Cota, Commander of the 28th Infantry Division, the generals had gathered. Besides General Cota, those present were the Supreme Commander himself, General Dwight D. Eisenhower, and next in rank, his 12th Army Group Commander, General Omar Bradley. General Courtney Hodges, Commander of the 1st Army and General Leonard T. Gerow, Commander V Corps 1st Army rounded out the group.[1]

The generals had assembled to investigate the rout of American troops of the 28th Infantry Division in their battle at Vossenach, the first objective in the battle for Schmidt, the ultimate objective. That rout, which had occurred two days, previously, on 6 November, was in actuality a disaster of such magnitude that it drew the top brass to the relatively safe basement command post of General Cota. The investigation of this day was simply a post mortem. What happened and what were the causes of the disaster?

What the generals heard in the inquest was shocking! Troops of the 2nd Battalion, 112th Infantry Regiment, 28th Infantry Division, situated on

---

[1] Charles B. MacDonald, *The Battle of the Huertgen Forest,* p. 119

the exposed northeastern nose of the Vossenach Ridge, had been shelled continually for four nights and three days by the German artillery situated on the Bergstein Ridge, which dominated the entire battle of Vossenach. Requests to be redeployed from the exposed ridge into safer areas elsewhere in the forest and into the village of Vossenach itself, where clear observation would be denied the enemy were turned down by a planning officer poring over a map. This officer had drawn a goose egg with a grease pencil over the nose of the ridge and that penciled goose egg became law.[2] Orders were orders! It was as simple and stupid as that.

The senseless slaughter of troops situated on an exposed ridge clearly seen by enemy gunners situated above them could make no sense to a private rear rank, let alone five generals hearing such testimony. Generals, knowing the awesome power of artillery and understanding the limits of human endurance, needed no further explanation of what happened in the shadow of the Bergstein Ridge on that fateful morning of 6 November, 1944.

The post mortem that took place in the command post of General Cota on 8 November, 1944 was the beginning of what would develop into the investigation officially recognized by the Office of the Chief of Military

---

[2] Charles B. MacDonald, *The Battle of the Huertgen Forest,* p. 97

History as probably the most thorough and meticulous investigation of any

single action in the history of war.[3]

WHAT THE INVESTIGATION DID NOT REVEAL

AND WHAT THE AMERICAN GENERALS DID NOT KNOW

The defense for the battle of Vossenach, the artillery placements atop

the Bergstein Ridge and, indeed, the entire battle for Schmidt were

personally masterminded by Germany's ace tactical commander, Field

Marshall Walter Model, who, being given up-to-the-minute details of the

battle while it was going on, prescribed all measures and counter-measures

employed in this strategic battle. Moreover, Field Marshall Model knew

that should the Americans reach and cross the Roer River at Schmidt, they

might take the Roer River Dams and that would jeopardize the execution

of the Ardennes offensive planned for mid-December, 1944.[4]

---

[3] R. W. Thompson, *The Battle for the Rhine*, (Vol. 2), p. 23
[4] Charles B. MacDonald, *The Siegfried Line Campaign*, p. 460

17773657R00176

Made in the USA
Lexington, KY
01 October 2012